SUPERSONIC SECRETS

SUPERSONIC
SECRETS

Written and edited by **Rob Lewis**
Contributing Editor: **Edwin Lewis**

Published by Exposé, a division of Secret Books Ltd.

Copyright © Rob Lewis 2003.

First published in the United Kingdom in 2003 by Exposé,
Secret Books Limited, 18 Bedford Row, London WC1R 4EB, United Kingdom.

Printed by Butler & Tanner Limited, The Selwood Printing Works, Caxton Road, Frome, Somerset BA11 1NF, United Kingdon.

ISBN Number 0-9546617-0-2.

A CIP catalogue record for this book is available from the British Library.

For further information or to order additional copies please see:
www.SupersonicSecrets.com

In memory of all those who lost their lives in Paris

Contents

Paris

1   **"Too late"**   13
     ... a day Paris will never forget

Early Days

2   **How it all began**   33
     ... the 1940s inventor who made Concorde possible

Supersonic Dreams

3   **A new chapter**   55
     ... how the supersonic story began

4   **Spies in the skies**   73
     ... the Russians decide to build a "Concordski"

5   **Boom time**   83
     ... or supersonic fiasco?

6   **Concordski returns**   91
     ... and the first French cover-up

7   **Supersonic marvel or white elephant with wings?**   103
     ... the Concorde team battle for orders

The Concorde Experience

8   **Flying with celebrities**   115
     "I only wish the flight had lasted longer"

Paris Revisited

9   **The Paris Crash: Jacques Chirac's lucky day?**   125
     ... and the truth behind the French accident investigation

To Fly or Not to Fly

10   **A Phoenix flies again**   147
     ... a new beginning? ... or the beginning of the end?

11   **Curtains for Concorde**   155
     ... and how the supersonics could have been saved

12   **Life after Concorde**   175
     ... will we ever fly supersonic again?

Written & edited by Rob Lewis

Contributing Editor: Edwin Lewis

Special thanks to:

John Bryant
Amanda Clarke
Viv Croot
Jonathan Crystal
Jane Deal
Cordy Griffiths
Graham Hayday
David Jones
Peter Jordan
John Lewis
Marina Papaspirou
Gordon Roxburgh
Anna Russell
Jetinda Sira

and

James Bedford
Gary Corbett
Paul Davis
Harry Evans
Corinne Jones
Mark Knight
James Hipwell
Magnus Macintyre
Alec Melville
Phil Sant
Catherine Scott

... and anyone else who has somehow been forgotten

Paris

Chapter 1

"Too late"

… a day Paris will never forget

July 25, 2000. As Jean-Cyril Spinetta headed off to work at Paris Charles de Gaulle airport it was clearly going to be another fantastic summer's day. What a shame then that the Air France president would be behind a desk, rather than basking in the glorious sunshine.

For Jean-Cyril there was absolutely no possibility of taking the day off. Forty-eight hours earlier a call had come through from a senior director at British Airways. This wasn't unusual in itself. BA and Air France spoke quite frequently - partly because they were the only airlines in the world to fly the supersonic passenger jet Concorde.

But the news from London wasn't good - and it meant Jean-Cyril Spinetta would be a busy man over the coming weeks.

The engineering division at Heathrow had discovered cracks in a wing spar of one of the British Concordes. There was no need for immediate panic - the cracks had been found in their early stages and did not seem to be a safety issue. However, they certainly raised some awkward questions.

When the supersonic aircraft were built it was originally expected they would fly until about 1993. A technical review later concluded that this "sell-by" date was rather pessimistic - the deadline for grounding was put back to at least 2010.

But could the cracks mean the decision to extend the working life was wrong? Perhaps there were other cracks too? And how confident could the engineers be that the problem wouldn't cause an issue in-flight? After all, the plane was put under uniquely challenging stresses and strains - every single time she flew.

Jean-Cyril made sure his engineering division took the issue seriously. The initial response from his team was along the lines of, "Well, we'll look at ours, but I bet we won't find anything wrong bearing in mind how those BA people look after their Concordes." Such competitive banter is commonplace in the industry.

But within hours, Air France's maintenance team realised they too had a problem. The cracks were tiny. None were visible to the naked eye. You needed ultrasonic equipment to detect them. But four of the six Air France planes had cracks.

Manufacturer Aerospatiale quickly inspected the fleets and decided that two of the supersonic planes had to be grounded. The engineering teams breathed a collective sigh of relief as the rest of the Concordes escaped the need for any serious repair. The supersonic flights to New York would continue, but as Jean–Cyril sat at his desk that day he could only wonder: "Yes, but for how long?"

❧

Ever since Jean-Cyril took the top job at Air France he had had one goal in mind: to turn the company around, to make it a modern profitable airline that could be fully privatised.

The Concordes were a potential obstacle to completing this mission. OK – it was very prestigious being one of only two airlines worldwide to offer passengers the ability to travel faster than the speed of sound. But the French supersonics made terrible losses. And unlike BA's planes, they didn't have permission to fly from London Heathrow, Europe's busiest airport. Without that there would be little chance of the Air France supersonics making money.

But commercial reasons alone would never be enough to get the Concorde fleet scrapped. The French nation still saw the plane as one of their proudest post-war achievements. Should Jean-Cyril propose to ground them for financial reasons, he would face national discontent. He would probably be the least popular man in France.

But mechanical failures, the rising cost of maintenance, doubts over airworthiness and unexpected cracks in the airframe... these were the kinds of reasons why Concorde could be scrapped without controversy. Perhaps it would be possible after all?

∽∘⌒∾

While Jean-Cyril worked at his desk, a flight dispatcher for Air France was organising the documentation for flight 4590, an Air France supersonic flight to New York. Though not the most glamorous job in the aerospace industry, flight dispatch is nevertheless essential. The complexities of a modern civil flight require hours of preparation, and while the pilots are able to perform all of these critical roles, confining their working hours to the cockpit gives more flying time and saves the airlines money.

The role of the dispatcher is to take all the information regarding runway conditions, aircraft limitations, number of passengers, baggage and fuel required, and check that everything is in order so that the flight can proceed as planned.

Flight 4590 was a charter flight for a group of holidaymakers on their way to a cruise ship that would sail shortly from New York Harbour. Almost all the passengers were from Germany, flying into Paris that morning.

The dispatcher groaned as he reviewed the data on his PC screen. This was going to be a very difficult morning. The plane selected was Concorde F-BTSC, the third production Concorde, and the oldest still in service. It certainly wasn't the

Concorde he had expected to use that day. The computer screen showed the original choice was suddenly "unavailable".

F–BTSC was just a backup.

The reason for the switch could only be guessed at. It could be as simple as a technician getting a bit over-enthusiastic with a spanner. It takes very little to do minor damage to an aircraft and, unlike their friends in the rail industry, aerospace engineers can't cover up problems with a short strip of gaffer tape.

But the computer showed the reserve aircraft also had a problem – something was wrong with the thrust reverser on Engine 2. This was not a safety issue as such – it was quite legal to fly with one thrust reverser broken. But to be able to abort a take-off, the pilot needed to be able to slow down quickly. The lack of full reverse thrust meant the plane would not be allowed to carry as much weight as normal.

And today's flight was heavy. Very heavy. It was going to New York with a full cabin of passengers, all of whom had enough baggage for a week or two with them. They would need lots of fuel for this trip, making the plane even heavier. The dispatcher's first run of calculations had showed that the maximum weight was exceeded by some 10 tonnes. As if that wasn't bad enough, repairs were being carried out on the runway normally used by Concorde and the length available to her had been reduced from 3,600m to 2,700m.

The flight dispatcher did his sums and took them to the duty officer. For half an hour or so they worked frantically through all the possible answers to the problem, from trying to get hold of a different aircraft to making a refuelling stop en route. They even considered sending the baggage to America on a different plane.

By 10am the anxious crew had got involved. The pilots were not too keen on any of the suggestions on offer, and took control of the flight preparations themselves. They were adamant that they must find a way to get to New York as planned - with no stops – and with all their passengers' luggage on board.

Taking over from a flight dispatcher wasn't too stressful, but it certainly wasn't the best start to a day's flying.

The crew came up with a simple but time-consuming solution. They would ask engineering to fix the thrust reverser. They would also seek permission to change to a longer runway. If they could get both these issues sorted out, the maths would just about work. The supersonic flight could go ahead as planned.

Permission to switch runways was quickly obtained but the reverser repair would take a while. The passengers would be in for an unexpected delay.

∼∾∾

Scrambling about under the wings of Concorde is no easy business for any technician, and working to a tight schedule brings unusual pressures. Normally a crew has days to get key parts replaced, as well as the benefit of a twenty-four hour shift system.

On checking the troublesome thrust reverser, the engineers discovered a small component called a Garrett motor was the source of the problem. It had definitely failed - and so the Air France maintenance men cannibalised the part from another Concorde to save time.

The installation was done right down to the letter. A test showed everything was in order and the plane was finally cleared for flight.

∼∾∾

Sitting in the Air France Concorde lounge sipping complimentary champagne was an old group of friends from Mönchengladbach, a small town not far from Düsseldorf.

The friends had been holidaying together for years. Initially it had been just a few couples, but with time the couples turned into families. This year thirty of them were embarking on a cruise on the *MS Deutschland*. It was currently moored in New York - and they would be sailing to Ecuador through the Panama Canal.

This was a very special trip. It had been arranged by Christian Stattrop, a local travel agent who was a close friend of many in the group. The *MS Deutschland* was something of a one-off and everyone felt Stattrop had come up trumps. The ship had all the modern comforts and safety measures, but was decorated in the style of a classic liner from the so-called golden era of travel by sea, before the aeroplane took over the long-distance travel market. The décor of this 'grand hotel' was said to show the great splendour of Edwardian style "with the ambience of the roaring twenties". Everyone agreed it was an ideal way to celebrate their first joint holiday of the new millennium.

As part of the package, members of the party were able to travel on Concorde to New York for a surcharge of just $1,500, less than half the usual asking price. Such an offer was exciting and rare – and added to the cruise, it meant a truly once-in-a-lifetime trip. But such was the popularity of the Concorde upgrade, Christian had had to ask his customers to draw lots to see who could go supersonic. In the end a lucky thirteen had ended up securing the supersonic upgrade. The remainder of the group were forced to take the rather less exciting subsonic alternative of a Boeing 747.

Amongst the thirteen winners were Kurt and Marion Kahle. They ran a local business school and were travelling with their eight year-old son Michel. Also flying were Harald and Silvia Ruch, who owned a security firm, and Werner and Margarete Tellmann, who had a well-known antique furniture business.

None of the holidaymakers had ever flown Concorde before so everyone was very excited, if a little nervous. As they sat in the lounge they were notified that there was going to be an unfortunate delay. But the free drinks would help pass the time and calm the nerves.

∽∾∽

Concorde boasted a crew of three in the cockpit – a captain, co-pilot and flight engineer. When the plane was built such an arrangement was quite normal for any large aircraft. The vast array of analogue dials and gauges in the cockpits required close scrutiny from three pairs of eyes.

However, modern passenger aircraft now had more advanced flight-deck technology, including intelligent instruments that could monitor the plane's systems and highlight the most critical data. This had enabled the cockpit headcount on many modern planes to be reduced to just two.

Concorde's cockpit was perhaps a little old fashioned in comparison - but experts agreed the inclusion of a flight engineer made her as safe as any 21st century aircraft. Another reason for the flight engineer was the elaborate Olympus engines, which could propel an aircraft weighing over 150 tonnes efficiently from 0 to 1,300mph, at times using afterburners. The only other planes with such a complex specification were fighter jets.

The captain on this day was Christian Marty, 54. Marty had clocked up some 13,500 hours of flight time in total - and had been flying Concorde for almost a year. He was a bit of a legend at Air France, having once hit the record books by windsurfing across the Atlantic.

The first officer was Jean Marcot, 50, who had more flight experience on Concorde than Marty, but had never made it to captain. He had been offered a captain post on a subsonic craft but turned the offer down - Concorde was the aircraft he loved.

The flight engineer was Gilles Jardinaud, also 50. Jardinaud had almost as many flying hours as the captain, and was no stranger to supersonic flight either.

These three were among the élite of Air France's personnel. In civil aviation, there was no greater accomplishment than to be on the flight crew of Concorde. Only the most experienced and capable ever made it.

Just before 1400 hrs the crew began work on the flight deck and the passengers were asked to board. Air traffic control had already agreed to the request for the full length of runway 26 Right. This was the middle of three parallel runways at Charles de Gaulle airport and the longest available that day. After a few minutes, air traffic control called Concorde by radio and gave clearance and permission to start up.

While taxiing to the runway the captain always discussed the procedures for the various different scenarios that could occur during take-off - and today was no different. Marty read back key figures and statistics and confirmed them with his crew, checking everyone understood what to do in an emergency.

Airlines have applied some simple rules to prevent a repeat of previous disasters. Up to an agreed "V1" speed, for example, the crew should always stop if they have any kind of failure. If a problem occurs beyond this speed, the crew should continue with the take-off anyway - and resolve the issue in the air.

∽◡∾

At 1400 hrs, flight AFR 4590 was finally given clearance by the tower to line up for departure. Whilst waiting for another plane to pass, the crew briefly discussed the fuel load and the centre of gravity. Both were critical to Concorde's safety. To ensure stability at take-off, the centre of gravity needed to be correct to within a very small margin - a couple of percentage points in the wrong direction and there could be a serious problem.

They also discussed a difficult issue - they seemed to be a little overweight, having not burnt up as much fuel during taxiing as they had expected. But they continued with the take-off arrangements anyway, despite being over their maximum structural weight.

As usual, the flight engineer also read out the brake temperatures - there was a maximum that couldn't be exceeded. Everything was fine today. The tower then provided the take-off clearance and wind direction, and the first officer read these numbers back in confirmation.

The captain then asked First Officer Marcot and Flight Engineer Jardinaud whether they were ready. All agreed that it was time to go.

There was now only one final and important task to carry out. The captain slowly read out what he wanted his first officer to say when they hit specific speeds on the runway. The first notification should come at 100 knots; "V1" (no turning back speed) should be called at 150 knots; "V-rotate" (when the nose should come up) at 199 knots; and a final call which would be at 220 knots, the speed Concorde would need to climb safely, even with one engine having failed.

With all this agreed, Captain Marty placed one hand on the engine controls. He then counted down, "Three, Two, One... Top".

With that he pushed all four throttle levers all the way forwards. It was time to go to New York.

The power of the four mighty Olympus engines was then unleashed from under the wings: Engines 1 and 2 in the left-hand nacelle, Engines 3 and 4 in the right. A thunderous jet of hot air erupted from the back of each nacelle, the exhaust glowing orange.

Concorde gathered speed tremendously quickly. The crew heard the gentle intermittent thud of the wheels crossing each join in the runway, the intervals between the thuds getting shorter and shorter.

Back in the cabin, the hundred passengers prepared themselves for their Concorde take-off. The acceleration in this supersonic plane was much talked about - it was as close as most passengers would ever get to the G-force and adrenalin rush experienced by a fighter pilot.

As the engines ran up to full speed, a secondary fuel cock automatically opened and jet fuel poured into the back of the engines. It lit instantaneously, and a sudden burst of thrust was felt. Afterburners.

Twelve seconds later, the flight engineer confirmed they had four reheats. Concorde now had maximum thrust and acceleration, with all engines running at 100%. The white centreline on the runway started to disappear under the nose faster and faster, the plane accelerating nearly twice as quickly as a Boeing 747.

It took only a moment for the co-pilot to call "100 knots", then eight seconds later he called "V1". There was no stopping the take-off now. Christian Marty moved his right hand from the engine throttles to the control column and prepared to take to the air.

So far everything that day had been routine. The systems were operating just as they had on hundreds of flights before. But in just a few seconds' time, everything would change. There were many factors in play, the most important being a small strip of titanium alloy 44cm long and only 1.4mm thick, which had just fallen off an American aeroplane. The titanium strip was the catalyst for what followed, a piece of metal that had no business being anywhere near Concorde.

On a runway 45m wide and 4km long, it was the most terrible misfortune that it had fallen on the width that Concorde's wheels were about to occupy - and also on the short length between Concorde's V1 speed and take-off.

Nor did this strip lie flat on the ground.

It had become bent and twisted, and this twist had enabled it to sit upright, its sharp edge glistening in the sun. The improbability of this positioning was akin to an act of God. On this unlikely sword, Christian Marty and 113 other souls were to fall.

The front right wheel of Concorde's left landing gear ran over the strip and there was a short, sharp noise audible throughout the cockpit and cabin, followed soon after by a change in background noise.

Back in the passenger compartment there was some confusion. It was less than forty seconds since the pilot had made an announcement of the impending take-off, which had quickly taken attention away from the in-flight magazines and safety cards. Whilst the more nervous flyers clutched the armrests for comfort, many believed the noise was just a perfectly normal part of a Concorde take-off. But they were wrong.

Some of the passengers in the back of the cabin would have felt the vibration and might have been alarmed. They would have had good reason to be concerned, had they looked backwards out of their tiny porthole window. Flames had appeared behind the underside of Concorde's left wing, streaks and fountains of flame.

The captain was aware that something was seriously wrong. He felt a drop in thrust and noticed the nose starting to veer off towards the left side of the runway. He started to make a correction with the rudder to try to bring Concorde straight again - but the plane wasn't reacting as he would expect.

Tyre failures were not that uncommon on Concorde and he probably assumed that this was the most likely cause of the problem. Marty began to gently pull back on the controls to try to bring the nose up. All the rules dictated he must continue with take-off. His crew were expecting him to do this - and any sudden change of plan could result in confusion - or even disaster.

But the plane was still veering left. Concorde was heading towards the grass, and fast. In the distance Marty could see another plane coming into view - they were now heading in the direction of a parked Boeing 747, and at an increasingly high speed.

First Officer Charcot had to think fast. Everyone in the cockpit had felt the bump a few seconds before and it was his job to scan the instruments and explain the reasons for it. He desperately needed to tell the captain anything of relevance, but there was no instrument that clearly explained the events of the past few seconds. He struggled to work out the exact cause. As the compass deviated further from the normal course, he instinctively called "Watch out!", surprised at what looked like his captain's apparent lapse of concentration.

Flight Engineer Jardinaud continued to stare at his panel and realised that something was seriously amiss. The two columns of instruments for Engines 1 and 2 were behaving very strangely, the dials swinging wildly up and down.

Like a general practitioner, a good flight engineer can diagnose certain textbook symptoms immediately. But he had never seen anything like this before. Jardinaud delved into his knowledge of turbojet engines but couldn't be certain what was going on. Perhaps an instrument fault? Maybe the problem was about to resolve itself? They were beyond V1 speed now and so would not be aborting take-off.

But he now had half of the engines showing signs of trouble, meaning Concorde was in peril. According to the manual, the plane wouldn't be able to take off with two of the four engines down.

∾∾

Back at his office, Jean-Cyril Spinetta heard a loud roar from the airport down below.

Concorde was much louder than the latest generation of wide-bodied jumbos. Despite Air France's difficulties, he always enjoyed seeing the graceful old bird take off just as much as anyone else. But as he got up to look out of his office window, his heart skipped a beat. The unimaginable was happening. Today's Air France Concorde service appeared to be charging down the runway in flames.

∾∾

Close to the other end of Concorde's runway was an Air France Boeing 747, recently arrived from Tokyo. After slowing down on runway 26 Left they had been waiting for permission to cross runway 26 Right to get to the terminal and offload the weary passengers. The pilot realised the flight's timing promised passengers the privilege of an excellent view of France's pride and joy taking off, and pointed this out to all aboard.

Those with keen eyes had already spotted it – it had started its engines some 4km down the tarmac. But many passengers on the Tokyo flight only noticed Concorde when its sleek white body was suddenly highlighted by a long trail of burning jet fuel.

A passenger took out his disposable camera and snapped an image that was destined to appear on the front pages of the world's newspapers.

～∞～

The situation was worsening on the flight deck of F-BTSC. Marty was trying to pull up the nose to take off – but was finding it increasingly hard to keep the craft on the runway. It seemed to be skidding out of control. Surely a simple burst tyre couldn't explain this?

And then a message from air traffic control: "Concorde zero four five nine zero, you have flames behind you."

The tower had neither a good view nor enough time to assess the likely cause. But a huge trail of flame was there. Where was it coming from? They had no idea. All they could do was ensure that the pilot knew of a fire.

On hearing these words, Marty's job became all the more difficult. An engine fire? A fuel leak? Burning tyres? He had spent days on the Concorde simulator but had never been put in this situation. He was now in test pilot territory.

He continued to raise the nose, to finish what he had begun. If he couldn't keep the plane straight on the runway, his alternative was to take his chances by getting it into the air. He was officially too slow to start raising the nose, let alone fast enough to attempt a full lift-off, but he continued to try to get airborne anyway.

The flight engineer was becoming increasingly concerned at further readings from Engines 1 and 2. Before him he could see both of his power plants behaving wildly and he simply couldn't decide whether one or even both of them required some form of action. If so, what on earth should he recommend? Realising the danger they were in, he muttered something that sounded like "Stop?". But six seconds later, the plane was in the air.

Concorde had been so far off the centre of the tarmac that Flight 4590 destroyed a runway edge light as it finally lurched into the air. The plane had narrowly escaped running off the runway and onto the grass reservation. But finally, Marty, his crew and one hundred passengers were in the air and had managed to gain a speed of 205 knots.

The fire bell sounded for Engine 2. The root cause of the problem was still unclear. Were the instruments correct? They had no idea. But knowing the potential consequences of ignoring an engine fire, the engineer reluctantly called out: "Failure Engine. Failure Engine 2."

Concorde crews are strongly encouraged to avoid shutting down engines when below 400 feet. This is to provide a margin for safety. But when his engineer reported the engine fire, the pilot didn't hesitate to have it shut down immediately.

But then Engine 1 began to fluctuate again. The pilot, crew and passengers all needed that one engine to survive, if only for a further minute or two. They were just 10km from the large neighbouring airport of Le Bourget.

The tower at Charles de Gaulle (CDG) had asked them if they wanted a direct return to CDG - but the captain had refused the offer. He knew Le Bourget was the best bet by far. They were struggling for speed and a big turn would be far too risky. They were also flying at just 205 knots and so treading a fine line between flight and disaster.

If only Engine 1 could hang on for a matter of seconds they could land safely at Le Bourget.

⌒⌒⌒

Down on the ground, Sid Hare, an American Federal Express pilot, was suddenly disturbed by an unusually loud aeroplane. What he saw would remain with him forever. A plane was "at two hundred feet above the ground... I can see it is in trouble. One engine obviously has had a catastrophic failure. It is trailing flames two to three hundred feet behind the airplane."

⌒⌒⌒

First Officer Jean Marcot was only too aware of the airspeed problem. Four times he had pointed out the reading - not trying to alarm the captain but to make him fully aware of the most important dial in front of him, now hovering at around 200 knots. By rights Concorde should have already fallen out of the sky.

To try to improve speed the captain ordered the undercarriage to be retracted. Jean moved the selection lever to up. But nothing happened. The gear wasn't working any more. Their problems were mounting - they would now need well over 300 knots to survive another engine loss.

Christian Marty would grip the controls for fifty more seconds, stretching out for Le Bourget airport as it slowly got larger in front of him. He and his crew had valiantly struggled to counter the problems that had beset them, but the fight for flight would be lost. At 14:44:11, Engine 1 failed completely. Nothing could save them now.

The strong, slender, sculpted wing of Concorde F-BTSC had tried its best to support the heavy load put on it, but the second loss of power heralded the end. A combination of weight, the asymmetric thrust and a lack of airspeed and power brought the plane crashing down to earth.

Marty's final words were simple. "Too late."

∾◡∾

Down at La Patte d'Oie, a small hotel in Gonessee, Alice Brooking, a 21-year-old student from Cambridge University, was in her room chatting to her sister on the phone.

Downstairs, the manager was holding a meeting with the hotel staff. The building was largely empty at the time, but they were expecting a large group to arrive by coach at any moment. But then Concorde struck the hotel. There was no warning. Michele Fricheteau, the hotel manager, suddenly felt a "burst of flame in the face". She escaped with another employee. Four others were less fortunate.

Alice heard the impact and ran to her room door to find the landing already covered in flames. She bravely jumped from her window and staggered from the fire shouting, "I'm alive, I'm alive." On watching the television news her sister in England – who had been left hanging on the phone - feared the worst. It would be some hours before her fears would be allayed.

There was no movement from the aircraft wreckage. For the 109 passengers and crew on the flight, the impact had been fatal.

∽∾

Tragically Christian and his crew had crashed just 2,000 metres off the threshold of the runway at Le Bourget. Had Engine 1 lasted for just 20 seconds longer they might well have made it.

Fire crews rushed into action. First to arrive were those from Le Bourget - but they quickly required the assistance of their better-equipped colleagues from CDG. It took hours for the inferno to be brought under control – there were nearly 100 tonnes of aviation fuel burning at the crash site.

The co-ordination of the rescue effort was performed in part by the tower at CDG, who had seen the events unfold. The staff stood stunned as Concorde struggled into the distance with a trail of flames behind it. They then witnessed the cloud of smoke that filled the horizon, something Fed Ex pilot Sid Hare later described as looking like a "mini atomic bomb".

Two minutes after the crash, the tower put aside what they had witnessed to deal with the remaining aircraft in the sky. There was a sombre message from air traffic control: "For all aircraft listening. I will call you back shortly. We're going to get ourselves together and we're going to recommence..."

∽∾

The investigation report that followed on 31 August 2000 implied that a single design defect was to blame for the tragedy. The conclusion was damning to both the aircraft and the generation of designers who had originally put her together.

The newspapers relayed the findings to their readers almost parrot fashion, believing it to be comprehensive. But careful investigation shows that the report was not quite what it seemed. Furthermore, this was not the first time that Concorde's real story had been kept from the public.

∽∘∾

Only a small part of Concorde's story is widely known. It is a story of innovation and courage but also of secret deals, cover-ups and tragedy. The following chapters document the brave efforts of the ingenious pioneers who made supersonic travel possible and provide detailed analysis of the tragic Paris crash - as well as exposing the real reasons behind Concorde's grounding.

This book is dedicated to revealing the truth, the real story of Concorde's Supersonic Secrets.

Early Days

Chapter 2

How it all began

... the 1940s inventor who made Concorde possible

The year was 1940 and Great Britain was under siege. Overhead, British pilots were desperately trying to regain control of the skies. A few hundred fighters of the beleaguered Royal Air Force (RAF) were pitted against four thousand or so fighters and bombers of the Luftwaffe. The Germans sensed victory. Invasion seemed imminent.

One of the RAF pilots was a man called Frank Whittle. He had a rather unconventional way of fighting the Nazis.

Frank didn't take to the controls of one of the RAF's Supermarine Spitfires or Hawker Hurricanes. Instead he worked all hours of the day in a small and rather ramshackle workshop in the little-known Leicestershire town of Lutterworth, desperately trying to turn an idea into reality.

Britain's resources were dwindling – not many people got to spend their years in a shed when they could have been flying an aeroplane.

But somehow, against all the odds, Frank Whittle had persuaded the government that he should be allowed to continue working on his great new idea, something called the jet engine.

Despite his inventiveness and enthusiasm, progress was slow. The government ministry dealing with Whittle had decided he should team up with a company called Rover.

Rover may have been good at hammering out tank engines. But it had no idea about Whittle's new invention, which required delicate engineering and the careful use of new alloys. It was not the kind of work Rover's metalworkers had any experience of. Delays, bad communication and a complete failure to realise that Frank Whittle was more than a mere eccentric meant progress was painfully slow. Months turned into years.

And then one day a new face arrived at Whittle's workshop.

Stanley Hooker worked for Rolls-Royce, one of the largest aircraft engine manufacturers in the land. At just 30, Hooker was already an engineering legend for designing a supercharger for the popular Merlin aircraft engine. The results were astounding. British Spitfires suddenly had a real edge over the Luftwaffe's fighters. They could move, turn, fight faster. The extra power Hooker had engineered meant the Germans were now beginning to fall from the skies over Britain in increasing numbers.

So this was Whittle's chance. Whittle explained his desperation. Clearly the Air Ministry was rather pre-occupied with manufacturing piston engines and cobbling together as many Spitfires as possible. But surely they should take a little more interest in his new type of engine? After all, he claimed, his "turbojet" engine could change the course of history. It could help win the war.

Whittle and Hooker drank tea and discussed the intricacies of the invention for hours. They didn't see eye to eye on everything, but they got on well enough. At times, the two Oxbridge engineers felt like undergraduates again. As the day drew to a close, they shook hands and Stanley Hooker wished the eccentric inventor good luck and said his goodbyes.

∽◦◦∼

A few days later, Hooker found himself describing Whittle's work to Rolls-Royce boss Lord Hives.

Suddenly it dawned on Hooker just how powerful the inventor had claimed his turbojet was. Whittle had said his early prototype engine delivered 1,000lb of thrust. This figure wasn't easy to compare with those of normal piston engines, which were generally described in terms of the horsepower of their propeller shafts. But Hooker eventually made the calculation – and he was completely stunned.

Down in Whittle's simple workshop was a prototype engine that equalled or surpassed the best Rolls-Royce could deliver. Rolls-Royce had an army of draughtsmen and engineers who worked day and night to improve its world-class engines. How could it be that something built in a shed could surpass all this engineering effort?

Lord Hives quickly arranged a visit to Lutterworth. It was not an opportunity to be missed. Perhaps this so-called turbojet engine could help win the war. If it really worked, Rolls-Royce couldn't close its eyes to such an exciting invention.

After seeing the somewhat limited facilities and the one and only engine, Hives remarked: "I don't see many engines – what is holding you up?"

Whittle shrugged his shoulders. There were problems in every area. Getting components machined was proving difficult. Subcontractors were completely unreliable.

Hives took charge. There was no time to be lost. "Send the drawings to Derby and we will make them for you." All the work would be done for free – and the mass production of the jet engine that would so revolutionise modern aviation had begun.

∽∾∾

But the new invention didn't have an immediate impact on the fighting. The technology was just too new – and for a long time there were no aeroplanes that could carry the engines.

Nevertheless, the tide of the war began to turn, largely down to strategic mistakes made by Germany. In June 1941, the British public cheered silently, as a second front opened up in the East –

Hitler had invaded Russia. The Führer may not have realised this was a mistake, but every British housewife did. Within a few months, there was even better news - the United States of America had joined in the fighting.

By now, the Rolls-Royce Merlin engines were famous. Many felt they had been instrumental in saving the RAF from disaster. But despite his company's achievements, Lord Hives was increasingly worried about its long-term prospects.

Come the end of the war, Britain would have a mammoth surplus of Merlin engines, which would all be sold for peanuts. Development could not save what would soon be obsolete technology. The days of making money from piston engines were soon going to be numbered.

Hives believed Rolls-Royce would only have a future if it focused on something new - and that had to be the turbojet business. But despite Rolls helping Whittle, the inventor was still tied to Rover, and the ties were seemingly impossible to break. So how could Hives get in on the turbojet venture?

He took the matter into his own hands by inviting the two brothers who owned Rover to dinner. Hives proposed a simple trade: A massive Rolls-Royce tank engine factory in Nottingham, in return for Rover's early-stage jet engine facilities.

The brothers quickly agreed.

Giving away the soon-to-be-useless factory in Nottingham is the sole reason Rolls-Royce survived - and today the company remains the premier supplier of jet engines worldwide.

There were others with foresight around - Sir Geoffrey de Havilland was one.

De Havilland's company had helped resolve two of Britain's biggest war problems - a shortage of aeroplanes, and the inability to build enough replacements when they got shot down. The biggest issue was airframes. They were slow to produce, metal workers were in short supply, and the large factories required for production were constant targets for Luftwaffe bombers.

De Havilland's novel solution was an all-wooden aeroplane. Not only could it be built by the army of otherwise unemployed carpenters, but the work could be discreetly distributed throughout the country to small workshops that remained hidden from the eyes of the German bombers.

When de Havilland's creation took to the sky it proved to be faster than any front-line fighter Britain possessed. The Mosquito was born.

∾∾

De Havilland had begun to build aeroplanes in 1908, inspired by news of the Wright Brothers' flight of 1903. He cheekily demanded a £1,000 deposit from his grandfather to be set against his inheritance. He spent the money on a series of early aeroplane experiments.

Against all the odds, Sir Geoffrey's home-made craft ended up participating in the First World War, winning him early public acclaim. By the early 1940s, he had built up a huge manufacturing business.

Sir Geoffrey was fascinated by Whittle's invention and his chief engineer Frank Halford spent hours examining the possibilities of the new turbojet. Halford quickly dreamt up the Vampire, an early aircraft specifically designed to utilise jet engine technology.

Sir Geoffrey had two sons, his eldest, Geoffrey, and 25-year-old John. Both were test pilots for the company, risking life and limb every day. Geoffrey Jnr was first to fly the Vampire in 1943. The journey went off without a hitch. It flew fast and smoothly, eerily so. On landing, Geoffrey told his father that "the smoothness is quite strange". The test pilot had been so used to the fierce vibrations of piston engines that he had found himself "tapping the instruments because there was nothing to vibrate them". Sir Geoffrey was heard to mutter that it was clearly "an engine for passenger travel".

∞✄∞

But De Havilland wasn't the only aircraft manufacturer getting excited about the Whittle invention. The British government had decided the US should have it, supposedly for the benefit of the war effort.

The prototype engine and Whittle's blueprints were loaded onto a Liberator bomber – and flown across the Atlantic. In a blink of an eye, Britain handed over a technological lead that would never help the Allied war effort, but would end up giving America a lead in aviation for decades.

The Americans were not slow in realising the potential.

After years of obscurity in Britain, Frank Whittle soon found himself invited to the United States. In an extraordinary whistle-stop tour in May 1942, he saw numerous plants and facilities, including those of Bell, General Electric and Northrop. The rate of progress astounded him. Facilities were state-of-the-art and much larger than anything back home. In just a few months huge jet engine factories – and production targets – had been set out.

Test flights of the first US jet, the Airacomet, began on October 2, 1942 – just one year and a day after the first US engineers had unloaded the new invention from the belly of the Liberator, and some five months before Britain's equivalent, the Meteor, ever reached the skies. Unlike Rover a few years earlier, the Americans hadn't hesitated to act on what was clearly a good invention.

∞✄∞

May 7, 1945. Berlin fell and the world rejoiced.

The fighting was over in Europe and large parts of the continent needed to be rebuilt from the ruins to give millions of soldiers, sailors, airmen and their families a peaceful future. In Germany there was much work to be done. The people had to be fed and democracy rekindled.

In Britain, the population was crying out for change, to create "a country fit for heroes". Even Winston Churchill was thrown out of Number 10 as the country decided to reinvent itself.

The end of hostilities left industry in turmoil on both sides of the Atlantic. After years of pumping out military equipment of every type under limitless government contracts, the priorities were turned upside down. The building of homes and hospitals was now paramount. Thousands of pieces of military equipment were also surplus to requirements, from jeeps and uniforms to rifles and second-hand aeroplanes.

Many an aeroplane factory closed its doors, realising that its days were numbered. Workers were laid off in the thousands.

⌒⌒⌒

Of course, the British government had been considering these post-war problems for years. The answer for the aeroplane companies, it was decided, was a committee. Lord Brabazon of Tara would be the chairman and the committee would direct the next generation of passenger aircraft, creating thousands of jobs. At least that was the theory.

The result of the Brabazon committee's endeavours was enormous amounts of public money being spent developing a plane called the Bristol Brabazon. This huge beast of an aircraft was designed to carry just 24 passengers in uncompromising luxury over a range of 5,300 miles. But it was clearly designed by a committee – it had a very peculiar shape, failed to exploit the benefits of the new turbojet engines and was so large that it could lumber along at only 250mph, guzzling fuel as it went.

The committee was finally forced to agree that the project should be suspended. Only one of the aeroplanes was ever manufactured, and even that never made it into service.

The Brabazon showed Britain that committees and planes don't mix. Sadly, the lesson wouldn't be remembered.

～∽ℭ～

By the late 1940s, the surviving aeroplane manufacturers had started to meet at a huge annual industry get-together, which took place in England, initially at Radlett and then at Farnborough. Everyone came, including the fledgling airlines. The manufacturers also brought their new planes along each year, in the hope of securing some orders. Many of the aeroplanes were flown in the skies above, to the delight of the assembled crowds. It was a time of real progress - new inventions and ideas were to be found aplenty.

But in both Britain and America there was general consensus on one issue. While innovation would continue, Whittle's turbojet wouldn't be on the agenda for passenger aircraft for years. Everyone agreed there were far too many technical hurdles to resolve. Some engineers talked of jet-based passenger planes being decades away.

So everyone was in for a bit of a shock at the 1949 Farnborough show, just four years after the end of war. Suddenly, out on the airfield was the world's first and only jet airliner, the De Havilland Comet. It claimed to be able to carry fifty or so passengers in comfort at twice the speed of any other plane in the world.

It was quite a shock.

Dismayed by the proposals of the Brabazon committee, Sir Geoffrey had gone it alone. In complete secrecy, he had ignored the experts of the Royal Aircraft Establishment and the many representatives of manufacturers and airlines. It turned out that he had established a Comet design team before the war was even over, in direct contravention of government guidelines.

But the project had come at quite a price for him personally. During the development period, both of de Havilland's sons had been killed while working as test pilots. One had died while flying close to the speed of sound, in an attempt to beat the world speed record.

∽∾∾

The new Comets were truly revolutionary. They represented a new and remarkable era of engineering. There were hundreds of novel features, including hydraulically powered flight controls with no manual backup - and high-pressure under-wing refuelling.

The greatest challenge for the Comet design was allowing the aircraft to fly high in the atmosphere. Only at an altitude of 30,000 to 40,000 feet would the air be thin enough to permit smooth travel at 500mph. Any lower, and the thirsty turbojet would have required too much fuel, and the aircraft would have been too heavy to get off the ground.

Enough work had been done during the war to produce wings that would work at that altitude - but accommodating passengers in comfort in the thin air was tricky. The simple solution, still used today, was a pressurised cabin. This made the chamber within the fuselage almost airtight, enabling the crew and passengers to remain oblivious to the conditions outside.

To make a pressurised cabin for an aircraft the size of the Comet was a major challenge. The secret of its construction was a special bonding technique De Havilland had developed for use with aluminium skins. Called Redux, it used an immensely strong and airtight adhesive to join the skin panels.

Equally revolutionary was the power plant - four turbojet engines discreetly hidden in the wings. No one had seen a plane that had looked like this before.

The Comet was a marvel. Britain rejoiced in being first, courtesy of Sir Geoffrey.

It was a day long in the coming for Frank Whittle, who had been labouring over his jet engine for almost three decades. At last, he saw his invention in commercial use. He was in poor health by now, suffering from the strains of years of development work, but he remarked: "The sight of the Comet in the air has done me more good than any doctors could do."

∽⊃⊂∽

The press were at Farnborough in their hundreds and the Comet hit the headlines with a bang. The American aerospace companies admitted they were startled – they had been well and truly beaten. Here was an aircraft ready for production that outdid anything they envisaged. Even on paper their prototypes couldn't compete.

Some US industry insiders heaped praise on the revolutionary plane. Others such as Cyrus Smith of American Airlines started a flood of criticism, focusing on the cost of the engines.

Much of the criticism was firmly extinguished after the plane's first flights. The Comet flew from London to Rome – and set a new world record. It then flew from London to Copenhagen – and broke the world record. Indeed, everywhere the Comet went it seemed to set a new world record, demonstrating the devastating speed of jet power.

A costing report revealed the Comet to be 20% cheaper than its nearest piston-engine rival. While more fuel was consumed, the greater speed allowed more flights to be completed in a year, thereby increasing returns. Airlines throughout the world quickly demanded their Comets. One French buyer remarked: "The rapid building of this British airliner has completely upset the world's plans."

∽⊃⊂∽

In the US, a storm was brewing. The American aircraft and engine manufacturers had spent vast sums on their own development projects, only to be beaten by de Havilland, who ran what was to all intents and purposes a small British cottage industry. How had it happened?

Newspapers talked of the world "halving in size". Travellers no longer had to consider long journeys in terms of days, but hours. Sir Miles Thomas, on a Comet sales trip to New York, observed: "When BOAC [British Overseas Airways Corporation, the forerunner to BA] gets Comets into service, New Yorkers will be able to take a swim in Bermuda and dry themselves at home."

This was just what Britain needed to ensure post-war prosperity. The country had sold almost all its foreign assets to America to fund the war. Its factories lay in ruins, its housing stock in tatters. It needed commercial success on an international scale.

And here it was, courtesy of a plane built by one of the UK's oldest manufacturers, one which had produced aircraft for two world wars. And what's more, it was powered by jet engines invented by an Oxbridge-educated RAF officer. The Comet could not have been a greater embodiment of Britishness had Churchill himself been at the controls.

❧

Having acquired a certificate of airworthiness, BOAC prepared to inaugurate passenger jet travel. On May 2, 1952, Comet G-ALYP (or Yoke Peter) left London for Johannesburg. A huge crowd turned out to see it off, including de Havilland himself. Just after noon, Yoke Peter left the ground and dragged the world into the commercial jet age.

But business did not come quickly from the big American carriers. Pan Am placed just three tentative orders, hopeful of Boeing delivering an American-built jet airliner in the near future. Heading the airline was Juan Trippe, a powerful figure in civil aviation. He saw the need for jet power - but wanted it from a home-made source.

On his desk he kept a model of the Comet in a shroud. When General Electric or Boeing came round to meet him, he would unveil it and tell them he wanted an American jet aircraft to buy and he wanted it fast - or he'd be buying the Comets in quantity.

∞◦∞

The Comet seemed very reliable. Piston-engined aircraft flew at a lower level, and had to deal with whatever weather they encountered. The vibration from the engines, the battering from wind and storms and the difficulty in navigating around high ground resulted in the loss of many aircraft. But the Comet was immune to such problems. Flying way up in the stratosphere, it flew above the weather, enjoying flight at an altitude even higher than Everest.

On the first anniversary of the inaugural commercial flight, Captain Maurice Haddon, 37, found himself flying Comet G-ALYV from Singapore to London with 43 passengers on board. Just days before the coronation of Queen Elizabeth II, the flight contained a number of VIPs from the Australian government.

Warned of bad weather ahead while refuelling at Calcutta, Haddon decided to press on and took off. Six minutes later he reported he was "climbing as planned" when suddenly the fortunes of the Comet took a turn for the worse. The plane fell out of the sky.

There were many eyewitnesses. Narayan Chandra Gosh saw a bright flash of light in the sky, and then stood in horror as the burning plane descended rapidly before splitting in two. He said he thought it had flown into an unusually violent storm.

International law decreed that the Indian authorities undertake the investigation. They eventually concluded the loss was probably caused by a severe storm.

Britain breathed a sigh of relief. Accidents through forces of nature were tragic, but not preventable.

∞◦∞

On January 10, 1954, war reporter and writer Chester Wilmot bumped into an old friend at Ciampino airport, Rome, a scheduled refuelling stop en route to London from Singapore.

Noel Monks was travelling with a party of journalists on a somewhat dated airliner, the Argonaut. Wilmot was on a Comet. Monks' aircraft was due to take off first – but Wilmot would get to London some two hours earlier. Wilmot tried to persuade Monks to join him on the faster aeroplane, but to no avail. Monks needed to stay with his group. He waved Wilmot goodbye and boarded the Argonaut.

Wilmot knew his friend would suffer hours of bumping through cloud, wind and rain – the Comet was an altogether more civilised experience. Soon enough the boarding announcement came in Italian. No matter which language you spoke, you couldn't fail to pick up the name, and people gathered round to watch the lucky few walk across the tarmac to the pride and joy of BOAC.

Captain Gibson went through the start-up Comet checklists and powered up his four Ghost engines. As his instruments came to life, he noticed hardly any change in vibration or noise. That was the beauty of the Comet – just a reassuring dull roar that crept slowly through the insulated cabin.

Moments later Gibson received clearance from the control tower and pushed open the throttles. Yoke Peter took off and began its steep ascent towards the stratosphere. Gibson reported his progress by radio. Almost twenty minutes after take-off, he was breaking through cloud tops at 26,000 feet.

Shortly afterwards he said he was over the coast and climbing to the cruising altitude of 36,000 feet. Captain Johnson in the Argonaut heard this report and asked Yoke Peter: "Understand you're passing (flight level) 260, what's the cloud cover over?"

Gibson replied: "George How Jig from George Yoke Peter, did you get my...."

His voice was rapidly drowned out by a second of static or interference and then silence.

Repeated efforts to raise Yoke Peter failed. She had gone.

Nineteen months after the Comet entered service, Comet G-ALYP - or Yoke Peter - had broken up in mid-air. On board were 22 adults, a girl of seventeen and six children. There were no survivors.

About twenty minutes after this last signal, Captain Johnson handed over control to his first officer - and walked back into the cabin to sit next to Monks. He sat there, pale and shocked for some seconds, before whispering: "I'm afraid your pal Wilmot has had it. The Comet has gone in. It is not answering our calls. Don't tell anyone." Monks absorbed the news soberly, kept the secret, and rode the bumpy three hour ride back to London where the press waited.

Sir Miles Thomas, chairman of BOAC, was told of the disaster immediately. After a flurry of interviews an investigation began. Some suggested sabotage or a bomb; others pointed the finger at De Havilland. But the Comet was now deep underwater - and this was long before the days of cockpit voice recorders or flight data recorders. The only evidence was a fleet of grounded aircraft.

∼∾∽

Engineers and technicians descended on the aeroplanes looking for potential flaws. No serious problems were found - but fifty minor modifications were still made. Hopefully these changes would make the Comet safer. By the beginning of March, confidence had been restored and it was again given a clean bill of health. On March 23, Captain Cane took off for South Africa with a full passenger load, bringing the modified Comets back into service.

But the confidence was short-lived. Just sixteen days later, on April 8, London heard reports that a Comet was overdue between Rome and Cairo. Yoke Yoke had succumbed in exactly the same circumstances as Yoke Peter, with a sudden disappearance about half an hour after take-off. Two hours later, Sir Miles Thomas grounded the Comet fleet again. Answers were needed - and the sooner the better. Winston Churchill - now restored as Prime Minister - personally ordered the investigation to be moved up a gear. The Royal Navy was ordered to find the wreckage in the sea off Naples, using all available ships and manpower. The scale of the task was colossal, but there was little alternative.

Two prominent investigators, Sir Arnold Hall and Dr Walker, also embarked on a remarkable experiment. A Comet was placed inside a large tank of water with its wings poking out through seals in the sides. Day and night, flights were simulated by filling the cabin with pressurised water and stressing the wings with hydraulic jacks to make them feel the loads of a craft. Once the tank testing had begun, the investigation team could only wait.

The salvage of Yoke Yoke slowly began to pay dividends. The wreckage was reassembled onto a wire frame of the size and shape of the original plane. Threads from the cabin upholstery and the perfect imprint of a coin were found on parts of the tail and aft fuselage. These clues suggested the cabin had been ruptured before the aircraft broke up - and before it hit the sea. The likelihood that the plane had suffered a massive loss in cabin pressure was increasing - but everything the designers knew said this couldn't have happened.

∽◦◦∽

Sir Arnold was just finishing breakfast one morning when the phone rang. It was the man on duty at the tank. "I think she's gone, Sir Arnold. The cabin won't hold pressure any longer."

Sir Arnold arrived at the test rig mid-morning. The tank had already been drained to examine the failure.

The metal skin had been ripped open over a length of eight feet - the origin was the lower rear corner of the escape hatch. Analysis showed that the cause was metal fatigue.

Fatigue is a process observed in metals when they are repeatedly subjected to loads, which are then applied and removed in cycles. Any piece of metal will finally fail – without warning – once a certain number of cycles have been performed. Modern material science allows accurate prediction of such failure, but in the 1950s understanding was based on pure empirical observation.

The Comets had crashed because of tiny stress concentrations that had been introduced when holes had been drilled inside the plane. The main problems were around the Comet's square windows – and near the plates for the aerials. The drilling had given these sections a very short lifecycle. Eventually a tiny crack would appear – which would then suddenly lengthen.

Metal fatigue has continued to be a problem, even today. In 1988, a Boeing 737 lost 18 feet of its roof due to metal fatigue – but amazingly only one person was killed. That incident was the result of poor maintenance and production complications.

In 1985, a Boeing 747 suffered explosive decompression following the botched repair of a pressure bulkhead. The loss of control that followed claimed some 520 lives. But generally, modern maintenance techniques and the introduction of ultrasonic and electromagnetic scans have helped eliminate metal fatigue problems.

❧

The full horror of what would have happened to the Comet passengers was presented to a public hearing, chaired by the influential Lord Cohen. The Comet's reputation was in tatters. It would take a long time for credibility to be restored.

But just a few days after Lord Cohen's report was published, BOAC announced that it had "decided immediately to instruct De Havilland to proceed with the building of a fleet of new Comets".

Meanwhile, some Comet 3's were modified. These airframes had been in production when Yoke Yoke went down – and their completion and sale was all that kept De Havilland from going under.

The Comets were put on route-proving exercises, which were as much about gaining public confidence as the aircraft itself. BOAC needn't have worried. Some may have been sceptical - but this didn't stop 35,000 people turning out to greet John Cunningham and his crew when they landed in Sydney, the first jet airliner to do so.

In other parts of the globe, the Comet received similar greetings. On a trip to Moscow, the renowned designer Andrei Tupolev admitted Comet was a "very beautiful aircraft".

At Hatfield, work was progressing on the brand new Comet 4, to be powered by Rolls-Royce Avon engines. The design was familiar, but a stretched fuselage doubled passenger capacity to up to 81. It was also stronger under the skin - and before production commenced it was subjected to rigorous testing, including a water tank test. Nothing was to be left to chance this time.

Sir Geoffrey and his staff were a little over-optimistic. They believed the Americans would take the better part of a decade to catch up with their efforts.

But the American industry had not lain dormant. When Boeing president William Allen saw the Comet at the Farnborough air show, he knew there was no point in waiting any longer. The technological leap had been made, and it was his turn to close the gap.

His company had many advantages over De Havilland. It had huge military contracts, massive facilities and Ford-style production techniques. One military project Boeing had taken on was the B47 Stratojet - a subsonic, high-altitude bomber. This government-sponsored project gave Boeing the engine layouts, control systems, material properties, pressurisation techniques and production methods required to quickly build its own state-of-the-art airliner, the Boeing 707.

⌒⌒⌒

Early in 1958, a new race began.

BOAC, Britain's largest airline, announced its intention to use the new Comet to operate a jet route across the Atlantic. The aim was to bring Europe and America closer together.

The Americans didn't want to be outdone. Pan Am responded by making a similar announcement. The only difference was that it would be using the new all American Boeing 707.

The British won the race on October 4, 1958, when Comet 4 G-APDC successfully flew from London to New York.

But the victory was short-lived. In the end, it was the Boeing 707 which emerged victorious. The Comet was an aircraft designed in the forties for the fifties. The 707 was a fifties aircraft for the sixties. The metal fatigue saga had cost De Havilland the opportunity to seriously develop the airframe or the engines. Innovation was held back by a fear that previous tragic events might repeat themselves.

Compared to the Comet, the Boeing 707 was a monster. It boasted a 135-foot wingspan compared to the Comet 4's 115 feet. It also seated 181 people, more than double the Comet's capacity.

Some airlines were quick to claim it was too large to fill, but Juan Trippe at Pan Am wasted no time in tabling his orders. He had been putting pressure on Boeing for years – and now he had what he wanted. The 707 would either be a huge loss or a mammoth success. He was happy to take the gamble.

The US eventually took the lion's share of the market. For companies such as Boeing, Lockheed and McDonald Douglas, the years following the Comet proved to be their most profitable ever. The Comet stayed in service, but orders were few and far between. Even BOAC eventually bought Boeing 707s. Operators faced a cruel choice – they could buy or die.

De Havilland's airframe business eventually merged with Hawker Siddeley, ensuring its survival. The engine division went on to become part of Bristol Siddeley. By the time Sir Geoffrey de Havilland died in 1965, he had done more for the economy, technology and prosperity of the country he loved than any man could hope to do.

~~~

As well as losing two sons, de Havilland suffered another terrible tragedy as he continued to push aviation boundaries.

At the 1952 Farnborough air show, military and civil aircraft from across Europe and the United States turned out to fight for the favour of the crowd. The latest De Havilland multi-role military aircraft was among the contenders.

The DH110 Sea Vixen was a supersonic evolution of a previous plane, the Swallow. John Derry and his observer Tony Richards put the craft through its paces at close to the speed of sound. It was a superb display.

Brian Trubshaw, the test pilot who would later fly the first British Concorde, was in the crowd with John Derry's wife. They viewed the display from the pilot's enclosure, impressed by the well-rehearsed manoeuvres which won much applause. Suddenly, as the plane approached the crowd at high speed, a dangerous phenomenon reared its ugly head - wing flutter.

This deadly vibration can be experienced at any speed, but is particularly dangerous at close to the speed of sound. It can shake an aeroplane to pieces in seconds.

This is exactly what happened. At that moment over Farnborough, the wing of Derry's Sea Vixen suddenly shattered - and the wreckage and engines flew into the crowd, killing 28 people and injuring 60 more.

As was customary at the time, the air show continued despite the accident, with the next plane in line being quickly passed for take-off. Derry's brave wife also stayed with Trubshaw for a while before finally being taken away via a back door. There was no chance of finding the pilot or the unlucky observer alive.

That was the day that Britain first learnt to associate a new word with danger and risk - "supersonic".

Supersonic Dreams

Chapter 3

A new chapter

... how the supersonic story began

On October 14, 1947, the World War Two fighter ace Captain Charles "Chuck" Yeager was strapped into an experimental Bell X-1 airplane, which was in turn slung into the hold of an enormous B-29 Superfortress.

As the B-29 took to the air Captain Yeager must have been rather nervous. He was about to attempt what many believed impossible - to travel beyond the speed of sound. Would this new experimental plane really be up to it? The engineers claimed the answer was yes, but many a pilot had died trying to accomplish this ground-breaking task. Even the manufacturer's own test pilot had refused this mission, demanding $150,000 danger money to even consider it. Yeager was put in the cockpit, his reluctant colleague quickly transferred to other projects.

As the B-29 reached her maximum speed at 25,000 feet, the experimental aircraft was dropped from her belly. Now it was all down to Captain Yeager, who had once famously shot down five Messerschmitts before tea time.

The X-1's rocket engine roared as Yeager accelerated closer and closer to the sound barrier - but he was beginning to feel violent oscillations. The plane was now shaking and the pilot felt he was losing control. The vibrations grew stronger and stronger. Could the plane really take it?

He was beginning to doubt it.

The faster he went, the harder things got. He anxiously watched the speed dial hoping for Mach 1, the speed of sound. Slowly the reading reached Mach 0.96, then 0.98. By now his vision was beginning to blur but he kept an eye on the instruments while concentrating on the horizon in an attempt to keep the X-1 running true.

And then suddenly everything smoothed out. The vibrations simply stopped and acceleration became easier.

On the desert floor, the world's first sonic boom ricocheted across the towns and ground stations dotted below. Some feared the worst, others gave a knowing nod to their colleagues. Yeager had taken a plane through the sound barrier for the first time. Shielded by a shockwave off the tip of the nose, like a bow wave on a ship, he was powering through the stratosphere.

A new chapter had begun.

∾ာ⌒

By 1956, the British aircraft industry had managed to replicate America's successes and had even broken the world airspeed record again with their new Fairey Delta, which could travel at a handsome 1,132mph (Mach 1.7).

Despite these advances, the British aircraft industry was in disarray. Global competition was fierce and many manufacturers were on the brink of financial ruin. The huge passenger planes being rolled out of American factories in Burbank, Santa Monica and Seattle were far superior to anything Britain could come up with.

And so it was that on November 5, 1956, a newly formed Supersonic Transport Aircraft Committee (STAC) met for the first time at Britain's Royal Aircraft Establishment at Farnborough.

On the agenda were a few simple questions. Could the British take a great leap forward by starting work on a supersonic passenger aircraft? If the military were requiring planes that could go beyond the speed of sound, wouldn't passengers soon do the same? And if Britain took the lead, could this new era help turn around the fortunes of a critical part of the country's economy?

One of the committee members was the famous aeroplane designer Dietrich Kuchemann, who had spent his early years designing Messerschmitt fighters for Nazi Germany. Towards the end of the war Messerschmitt had produced truly state-of-the-art aircraft, including the radical jet-powered Me-262, which fortunately saw little action, largely due to the country's lack of fuel.

Kuchemann and several of his Me-262s had been secretly transported to England and by now the German designer was seen as a leading light in British aircraft design.

What Kuchemann proposed to the committee was a revolutionary concept - a huge, supersonic passenger aircraft with slender delta wings. According to the ex-Messerschmitt man the design would be efficient at supersonic speeds while performing admirably at landing speeds. The wings would need to be very thin and carefully sculpted to maximise their aerodynamic capabilities. But Kuchemann claimed they could provide a fast, efficient, safe and reliable supersonic plane.

The design, with its thin, triangular wings, looked rather like an ordinary paper aeroplane, but this didn't stop the committee getting rather excited.

But their enthusiasm was short-lived when some recent American research was brought to everyone's attention. It had only just been published and didn't bode well. A well-regarded US research lab had concluded that deltas were highly unstable under certain critical flight conditions. This phenomenon had been christened "Delta Roadblock" and seemed to make the prospect of supersonic passenger travel ever more distant.

∾◦◦∽

A World War One pilot-turned-engineer was determined to prove the committee wrong. W. E. Grey produced some outstanding work - but got little recognition. Indeed, no one even remembers his Christian name.

The passionate Mr Grey tried to save the supersonic programme by setting up a series of experiments using different delta shapes, which were then fired from a catapult.

Initially, he wasn't allowed to use Farnborough's extensive wind tunnels but instead placed the catapult on top of a stepladder, and used a camera to record the results. As his work progressed, he graduated from the stepladder to the roof of a Farnborough balloon shed and then eventually onto a helicopter. Finally, he was given the keys to the wind tunnels and a test plane, the HP115, was constructed.

Grey's results were astonishing. The Americans had got it wrong. Not only was the delta quite stable, it was actually more stable than a conventional plane.

An air of excitement spread over Farnborough. The biggest problem for a supersonic transport (SST) was the aerodynamics - and the Kuchemann design seemed to solve everything. There were other benefits too. A delta wing would be much more robust than a traditional wing and help keep the weight down, making the plane more economical to run.

It was a great chance for Britain. Once again there was the opportunity to lead the world through innovation, just as it had done with the Comet.

In March 1959, the STAC presented its findings to the controller of aircraft at Britain's Ministry of Aircraft Supply. The STAC put development costs at between £75 million and £95 million for a long-range SST.

But the estimates were wholly unrealistic.

They would come back to haunt the plane's designers in the years to come.

~∞~

Duncan Sandys was Britain's Minister of Aviation at the time and as he sat at the Cabinet table in Downing Street he couldn't have put his case more bluntly. "If we are not in the supersonic aircraft business, then it's really only a matter of time before the whole British aircraft industry packs in. It's obviously the thing of the future… We cannot afford to stay out." The argument was persuasive and the Cabinet didn't hesitate to sanction the funds required for some preliminary studies.

But Sandys had other challenges. He knew that the country couldn't support the dozen or so competitors that had somehow survived since the war, and he was keen to see some mergers take place to consolidate the industry.

The prospect of a supersonic contract was just the carrot he needed to force arch-enemies together. A few months and many corporate marriages later, Britain had only two major aircraft manufacturers - Hawker Siddeley and the British Aircraft Corporation (BAC). The Bristol division of BAC won the contract to start work on the long-range supersonic. Hawker Siddeley started to develop a short-range version - but it would never see the light of day.

Powerful engines would also be vital to the project. A supersonic plane was going to need some extraordinary thrust. For years the military had used a powerful jet engine called the Olympus, later to be acquired by Rolls-Royce, in its top-rated jets. Fitted for many years on the British Vulcan bomber, it was already being upgraded from 10,000 to 20,000lb thrust. The engineers believed it could be pushed even further.

❧

Over in France, President de Gaulle had his own supersonic ambitions. Believing the "American colonisation of the skies" needed to be challenged, Sud Aviation of Toulouse had been charged with coming up with a supersonic aircraft for France.

Sud had been a remarkable commercial success in recent years. Despite the French aircraft industry's almost complete obliteration in the war, Sud had somehow managed to create the Caravelle, a jet-powered medium-range airliner that had successfully challenged the otherwise dominant Americans. It had sold in the hundreds - and had even been bought by some American airlines.

But a supersonic airliner would require a quantum leap in technology and Sud's engineers knew they faced considerable challenges. A supersonic "Super Caravelle" would require new hydraulics, new electrical systems, new wing materials and new air-conditioning systems. Indeed, almost every detail would require a technological leap.

They couldn't do it alone. Slowly but surely a dialogue started between Sud's engineers and those across the channel at BAC. Initially there was no intention of creating an aircraft together. The talks were merely a recognition that they faced common difficulties and could save money by working together.

∽∾∿

By 1961, the British Prime Minister Harold Macmillan had decided upon a radical new strategy for the country. In essence, he would give up Britain's ambition to be a go-it-alone world superpower and focus instead on integration into the ever more important European Economic Community (EEC).

Unfortunately for Macmillan the French were hostile, believing Britain would spoil the new economic union. Britain would have to pull out all the diplomatic stops if the French vote could be counted on.

Macmillan decided he needed a real-life demonstration of true British Europeanism, a case study which would seal a British application.

If General de Gaulle saw the UK throw its weight behind a joint Franco-British supersonic project, for example, surely he would give Macmillan the keys to Europe? After all, in so doing Britain would be putting its aeronautical future in the hands of the EEC.

So Britain's new Minister of Aviation Julian Amery was given a mission. His boss at Number 10 wanted to get BAC and Sud to work together on a common supersonic aircraft - and to get the French government to pay for half of it in the process. It was a difficult task that would require lobbying, cajoling and hundreds of meetings.

Amery sounded out the French government and discovered they would be supportive; but when it came to the companies themselves, it wasn't so easy. The two design teams even disagreed on what a supersonic plane should look like. For months the two sides bickered.

∾◦∾

Bored of protracted and ineffective meetings, Sud Aviation's senior designer Lucien Servanty decided to go it alone. He would directly approach the only person who really counted. Ignoring protocol as well as his appointments for the day, he unexpectedly turned up at the reception desk of the Paris hotel where his counterpart was staying. He demanded an urgent audience with Dr Strang of BAC and then bluntly informed the Briton that he would be taking him for a spin in his company Citroën.

The two engineers didn't have much in common. Servanty was a grizzly, chain-smoking Gaul; Dr Strang a rather dry and clinical accountant-like figure. After a scary high speed drive through the back streets of Paris, Dr Strang found himself at an old aerospace factory at Suresnes.

Servanty informed his guest that they would now be locked away alone in an office until they reached agreement. Many hours passed in that smoke-filled room. Doubtless a few drinks were consumed too. As the pair sketched out draft after draft of what a new joint supersonic airliner could look like, their colleagues were becoming increasingly concerned about their absence at the official negotiations.

By the end of the day, the two designers had finally reached an agreement. The sketches were copied, signed and sent back to their startled colleagues. Strang would later comment that the experience had reminded him of his schoolboy days.

Servanty and Strang's work enabled a long-awaited joint draft design for a joint supersonic to be created - and a sketchy specification was soon laid on the desks of the British and French ministries. The development budget was roughly estimated at £150 million or so, which was to be shared equally.

❧

Behind the scenes, Sud's French engineers were praying that the deal would go through. In hushed whispers, they discussed the importance of the Olympus technology. It would be critical if they were to get a supersonic aircraft in the air. The French manufacturing operations were years behind and only a joint project would give them the blueprints for the famous engine. For France's aerospace industry, the deal would be ground-breaking.

For Macmillan the benefits would be largely political. He would have his example of European integration, a project that would hopefully give Britain a passport into the EEC. With a bit of luck, he would go down in history as the PM who had successfully negotiated the UK's entry into Europe.

❧

Julian Amery and the French ambassador Geoffrey de Courcel finally signed the international treaty to develop a joint supersonic aircraft on 29 November 1962 at Lancaster House in London.

It was a remarkable agreement in more ways than one. No responsible company would ever have signed it. Here was a 50:50 joint development project with an open-ended, multi-million pound cost - but no detailed specification. In effect, both countries were agreeing to pay 50% of whatever the costs ended up being.

And worst of all, there was no break clause, no provision whatsoever for scrapping the project should it go over budget or fail.

Amery had insisted on the absence of a break clause. Suspicious of the French from the start, he had believed they might one day change their minds.

It was a treaty that would come to cost the British and French taxpayers an awful lot of money.

∾∾

The Elysée Palace is the official residence of the President of the French Republic. It was a particularly busy place on Monday 13 January 1963, with almost a thousand journalists clambering for positions in the huge auditorium.

President de Gaulle was to give a rare press conference – and according to the rumour mill everyone was going to walk away with a very good story that day.

For over a year, Britain's top politicians had spent every waking hour trying to ensure a successful entry into Europe for their Prime Minister. Would this be the day that France finally acknowledged Britain had won its right to join the club of EEC nations?

The room quietened as General de Gaulle arrived and walked slowly to the stage. The TV cameras and microphones followed his every move.

It was not to be Macmillan's day.

Britain, de Gaulle quickly informed the audience, was not yet ready to accept the EEC "without restriction, without reservation". France, he informed the journalists, would veto the application for membership. There was the possibility of re-considering the issue in the future, he admitted, if "Britain's own evolution of the universe" was to bring it closer to the continent.

And then, to everyone's surprise, de Gaulle unexpectedly christened the new joint aerospace project which until now had received only limited publicity. "Nothing," he said, "will prevent the close relationship and direct cooperation, as these two countries have proved, by deciding to build together the supersonic aircraft Concorde."

This was the first time the Concorde name had been used publicly. The ten-year-old son of a BAC official had come up with the name – but no one had actually expected it to be used. Somehow the idea had reached the Elysée Palace where it had grabbed the President's imagination.

Sadly for the British Prime Minister his submissions had been given somewhat shorter thrift than the ideas of the inventive ten-year-old. This was a very public humiliation for Prime Minister Macmillan, who would find his party dispatched from 10 Downing Street following a rather painful electoral backlash only two years later.

∾◦◦∾

Ask a management consultant how to run a company well and he or she will probably give you a few basic pieces of advice.

For a start, make sure you have strong leadership. Put one person in charge: the chief executive officer (CEO) should make sure things happen. He or she should also ensure the company is run efficiently with no duplication of effort, with clear budgeting and cost control at every level.

Below the CEO there should be a simple and easy to understand management structure where every key executive understands exactly his or her responsibilities. It is imperative that the whole company has a simple and well-understood goal.

Of course, there may sometimes be the need for discussion or debate between colleagues – and when this is the case it is best to try to keep such meetings small.

If there was ever a development project to prove why management consultants come up with such guidelines it was Concorde. Every rule in the book was broken; every potential for efficiency ignored. Concorde was an expensive case study of how not to manage a modern business.

For a start, the original budget of around £150 million was drawn up based only on a crude sketch and a six-page contract. When the estimate was signed off, the British and French teams hadn't even fully agreed on what they were trying to build.

It would take several years before the French admitted Concorde would be designed for long haul. For nearly half the project they believed they were building something for short-haul routes, such as London to Paris.

To compound the problems, the project lacked a proper CEO. Instead, there were a series of over-sized committees, none of which benefited from proper leadership. In the interests of "fairness" the chairman of each committee would be French for two years, then British for the next two, and so on. Decisions were slow in the making and frequently overturned.

To make matters worse, all contracts were to be allocated based on a strict 50:50 split between France and Britain. As a result, the committees were often unable to select the best supplier if they happened to be based in the wrong country. This led to bitter arguments.

Ironically, the very civil servants desperate to keep financial control were the ones to impose this gross inefficiency and organisational chaos, and it didn't take long for the normally entrepreneurial manufacturers to become disillusioned. Sir George Edwards of BAC would later claim that costs could have been at least a third less without the form-filling government officials.

And so the expenses mounted. The French team were not greatly concerned – General de Gaulle had made it clear this was a project he would see to fruition, whatever the financial consequences. Millions of taxpayer's francs continued to be supplied without hesitation.

But on the British side of the Channel the development teams were in for a far harder battle. Fleet Street was only too happy to regurgitate a rather revealing report, published by the Committee of Public Accounts (CPA), an important House of Commons watchdog. For the first time, the public discovered that the £150 million development budget had been nothing more than a guess, and that the Treasury had failed to take any part in ensuring the numbers added up.

Worst of all, the CPA exposed a complete failure to analyse the potential return on investment. Supposedly the logic for this mammoth undertaking was that if the Concordes sold for "£3 million to £4 million each" and "150 to 200 aircraft were sold... we might be able to recover a good deal of the money".

The government grew restless. Within a couple of years of the treaty being signed, the budget had already doubled to £300 million. It would eventually top an astounding £1 billion, almost eight times the original estimate.

∽∾∾

By the time Harold Wilson took office in 1964, Britain was in grave economic difficulties. An £800 million deficit in the government's finances left many a Cabinet minister wondering how the country's books could ever be balanced. Officials talked of half-built schools being abandoned and hospitals being closed down at short notice.

On Monday 19 October, the new Labour Prime Minister and his Secretary of State for Economic Affairs George Brown sat down and without hesitation recommended the scrapping of a large number of important government projects. The revolutionary British TSR-2 supersonic bomber, which was already flying, would be consigned to the scrap heap. Concorde, which was still some way off but showing progress, would also die.

The reason? Brown believed Britain could obtain American dollars to prop up the UK economy - but only if these aerospace developments were quietly terminated.

Within days the Americans had agreed to the deal. Yes, it was callous. But if the British ditched these projects, putting thousands of British workers on the dole, the Americans saw a bright future, a future filled with additional aerospace contracts from Britain. The US administration felt Brown's proposal was a deal worth doing – a few hundred million dollars to shut down the British competition.

Sadly for Wilson and Brown, no one had taken the time to read the original Concorde contract – and the over-inflated egos in the Cabinet had failed to consider a consultation with their Parisian partners. Leaked stories of a Concorde cancellation soon reached the front pages of London's newspapers. The British public read the stories with alarm – and so did the French government.

The French were absolutely incensed. There had been no official warning or briefing of a potential problem. The way in which this had been handled was considered an extraordinary breach of diplomatic etiquette. What's more, de Gaulle sensed the American involvement in the plan. The French President was a very unhappy man indeed.

The British PM dispatched Roy Jenkins, the latest Minister of Aviation, to Paris. Jenkins was not in for a smooth ride. His French counterpart Marc Jacquet refused to countenance cancelling the project. The idea of restricting development to prototypes was also canned. A British proposal to share development with the US was laughed at, and a handover of the project to France was dismissed.

And then, suddenly, just as the meeting looked like it was closing, Jacquet rose to his feet and angrily waved the treaty in the air, reminding the British that in case they had forgotten there was absolutely no possibility of withdrawal. It was an international treaty, the costs were to be shared 50:50. Concorde would go ahead as planned – and the British would pay their half share.

It didn't take long for the new resident of Number 10 to realise he was cornered. Amery's decision to leave out a termination clause had been designed to prevent the French walking away mid-term. The attorney general Sir Elwyn Jones was asked to review the legal position and came to a simple conclusion. Britain couldn't possibly exit the Concorde project – the French would sue and win damages of hundreds of millions of pounds.

The British Cabinet's resolve soon crumbled. Concorde was saved, not by negotiation but by Julian Amery's early mistrust of the French.

Of course, the Anglo-French project wasn't the only show in town. Slowly but surely, the Russians and Americans decided that they too might need a supersonic passenger transport.

Whilst developments in the USSR were kept largely under wraps, US efforts were somewhat more public. President Kennedy commissioned a report on the possibility of a supersonic passenger plane to compete with the Europeans.

Initially the American efforts were somewhat feeble in comparison. Despite being years behind Concorde, the US budget for initial research was just $11 million. The sum was paltry, certainly compared to the billions being spent by NASA trying to get a man on the moon. The American administration seemed to be quite happy to come last in this particular race.

Juan Trippe, the president of the Pan Am airline, changed all that.

Charming and well-educated, Trippe was regarded as a ruthless visionary. In the late 1950s, Pan Am had forced Boeing to progress jet aircraft by threatening to buy the British Comet. Later, the company's large-scale purchase of Boeing 707s had forced competitors to ground their fleets of piston-based planes. Trippe was a powerful man – the industry watched his every move.

Trippe quickly became convinced that supersonic was the future – but he was also worried that this would be a one-horse race with the Anglo-French Concorde having a monopoly of the skies. In his view, the American players had to get their act together. They had to catch up with the Europeans and they had to start doing it soon.

By the early sixties he had decided it was his own personal responsibility to get the American manufacturers to commit to a supersonic race. Being rather unconventional, he did this not by sending his right-hand man to Washington to lobby, but by despatching a negotiating team to London.

✺

Concorde's design had advanced significantly by now. The specification was still far from certain, but in every area from airframe to air conditioning and engines, the design team had made real progress. But she wasn't flying yet. There wasn't even a full-scale prototype to show. So it was a major surprise when Pan Am suddenly announced it wanted to buy a fleet of supersonic planes as soon as possible.

Pan Am contracted to option six Concordes. These options were fairly meaningless commercially – in effect, Pam Am was simply reserving a place on the production line in return for a small deposit. But it gave everyone involved an illusion of a sale. Concorde looked like it had won its first orders.

The news caused real excitement among the Concorde manufacturers and it was a big shock for the American President. If the American airlines were already starting to get their cheque books out, then perhaps the US needed to treat the supersonic race more seriously.

The day after Pan Am's option announcement, JFK stunned the world by announcing that supersonic development was now to be top of his political agenda. "Congress should be prepared to invest the funds and the effort necessary to maintain the national lead in long-range aircraft... spurred on by the competition from across the Atlantic."

It was an impassioned speech and exactly what Pan Am's boss had been hoping for. By spending a few thousand dollars in option fees in England, he had forced the US President down a road that would lead to hundreds of millions of dollars of taxpayers' money being put into supersonic research and development. What Trippe didn't let on was that Pan Am was only ever really interested in a home-grown supersonic.

∽◌∽

It didn't take long for the American manufacturers to get carried away.

In late September 1966, press and airline representatives were invited to Boeing's development labs in Seattle to witness the unveiling of the Boeing 2707-200, "The Boeing SST". Many of those attending remarked that the event was reminiscent of a Hollywood set - there was nothing that could actually fly, but there was a $2 million full-scale mock-up of what a plane might one day look like - and enough illumination to put a Broadway show to shame.

Boeing claimed their supersonic aircraft would fly at Mach 3 (2,000mph) using an airframe made of steel or titanium, easily beating Concorde's intended top speed. Seating between 250 and 300 passengers seven abreast, every industry guru realised this was the first real threat to the Anglo-French venture.

Like Concorde, the Boeing prototype sported variable nose geometry to improve flight deck forward views on approach. But the wing design was completely new - they would change angle during flight. This exotic feature would let the American variant take off and land at slow speed, even on short runways - a major advantage over a fixed wing aircraft like Concorde.

As the assembled masses looked on in awe, the Boeing PR officials knew there were lots of unanswered questions. Many of the design elements, particularly the adjustable wings, were based on untried technology.

But the guests were easily distracted from asking too many difficult questions. The model was impressive, as was the comfortable interior. There were new types of seating - and a novel in-flight entertainment system. Retractable TV screens were sited in the overhead luggage racks every six rows. Each pair of first class seats also sported a dedicated TV screen.

Boeing predicted that the first flight could be made in early 1970 with airline service by mid-1974.

In reality, the Seattle company had bitten off more than it could chew. The requirement for Mach 3 travel meant the skin had to withstand long periods of time at 260 degrees Celsius. The movable wings needed to be mounted on huge titanium bearings, which had never been done before. Most critically, the new wing design created weight issues that the designers would never be able to solve.

After 30,000 hours of wind tunnel research and 8.5 million engineering man-hours, Boeing was eventually forced to give up on the project and admit that the plane couldn't fly. Over one billion dollars had been frittered away on a wholly unrealistic dream. The Boeing SST never even got to the finished prototype stage.

Over in Europe, Concorde's development continued apace. With most technical issues now resolved, the Anglo-French consortium started to build their prototypes, believing they were now certain to win the supersonic race.

Chapter 4

Spies in the skies

... the Russians decide to build a "Concordski"

In 1953, Nikita Khruschev took over from Stalin as premier of the Soviet Union. With his appointment, the Cold War cast an ever-darker shadow over Europe.

A few years later, dignitaries and press stood on the tarmac at London Heathrow, preparing themselves for a good dose of Communist rhetoric. The new First Secretary was coming to London for a key diplomatic conference.

Everyone was used to Soviet leaders arriving in rather ancient 1930s propeller aircraft. Such craft must have been rather embarrassing for the leaders of a supposed world superpower.

So there were gasps from the crowd when Khruschev suddenly landed at London Heathrow in a huge new aeroplane, the first Soviet jet airliner: the Tupolev TU-104.

This was only the second passenger aircraft in the world to be powered by the jet engine - Western experts had assumed that the Soviets were decades away from such an achievement. Against all the odds, the USSR had followed Britain to enter the next generation of air travel. They had even got there before the Americans.

What made it all the more embarrassing for the British was that the British Comet was currently grounded due to safety concerns.

Britain's new monarch, Queen Elizabeth II, watched the plane land. She couldn't hide her curiosity – and the Soviet leader was delighted to give her his views. It was, he said, "an excellent plane – very modern; undoubtedly the best in the world."

The value in propaganda terms was immense. The Soviet Union had beaten America at its own game. For the leadership, the Tupolev was worth a thousand issues of *Pravda*. The mighty four in the US – Boeing, Lockheed, MacDonnell Douglas and Northwest – couldn't believe it. It was bad enough Britain beating them in the jet airliner race. But the Soviets as well?

In truth, the TU-104 lacked many of the technical refinements of its Comet equivalent. But this didn't stop it becoming a best-seller in the Communist East. Over 200 were eventually built.

❧

The man responsible for this industrial miracle was Andrei Tupolev.

Andrei was a legend. In 1918 he had apparently marched uninvited into the Kremlin and persuaded an amazed Lenin to build a Central Institute of Aerodynamics. He had been just 30 at the time.

In the early days of Communist Russia he became a popular figure, overseeing the design of hundreds of aircraft, all of which bore his name. But one day he made a costly personal mistake. Some of Tupolev's engineers had been arrested on charges of subversion. Tupolev responded by issuing a formal complaint, not the best idea in the uncomfortable political climate. He was quickly arrested. Fabricated charges of high treason were made – and he was sentenced to death, although Stalin relented and commuted his punishment to life imprisonment.

As the famous young aerospace engineer disappeared from public view, his aircraft were suddenly repainted and renamed.

But the fanatical designer refused to give up. For years he drew up successful aircraft designs from his prison bed. Some ended up in production, including war-winning aircraft that fought valiantly against the Nazis. He was finally released, along with the engineers he had originally sought to help. Tupolev got his job back and even received an apology from Stalin.

Tupolev went on to design hundreds of civil and military aircraft. His skills were very different from those required by a US aircraft designer. Mass production in the USSR was only possible through simplicity of design and the mass application of elbow grease - it was a country with a wealth of natural resources but severely limited industrial technology.

In the West, Tupolev was admired and liked. Sir James Harrison, who would go on to design the wing of Concorde, believed that, "Tupolev was the king of the Soviet aviation industry. He was the grand old man."

∽∾⌒

Khruschev was delighted with his reception at London Heathrow. Andrei Tupolev would now be at the helm of all important Communist aerospace projects. One such opportunity emerged when news of the Concorde initiative reached Khruschev. The Russian leader would not be outdone - he thought it his duty to beat anything the West could come up with.

So Khruschev gathered the aviation engineers together for a top-secret meeting. Just as the TU-104 had competed with the Comet, so too would a Soviet aircraft compete with Concorde. But this time, Khruschev had his heart set on the USSR coming first in the race. Design outlines and specifications were to be immediately drawn up for a Russian supersonic aircraft. It would be called the Tupolev 144 or TU-144. Andrei Tupolev would be chief designer.

∽∾⌒

Tupolev knew he would have to opt for a delta wing, just like the French. But he had no existing research data or experience of deltas. As Concorde's design began to gather momentum, Tupolev realised he had a big timing problem. He needed to accelerate research and overtake the Anglo-French consortium. But how? He turned to the most devious of methods – the KGB.

Tupolev had no intention of copying Concorde outright – but the more he knew about his competitor the better. Like a sneaky schoolboy, he decided his job would be considerably easier if he could only get hold of someone else's homework.

∽∾∽

In 1963, shortly after the original Anglo-French agreement was signed, a British delegation that included Aviation Minister Julian Amery was invited to Moscow. To their amazement they were shown a model of a proposed Soviet SST. There was a striking resemblance to Concorde – the British exchanged glances, suspecting espionage.

They were right – a vast network of spies and foreign workers had already been established for the cause.

Russians living or working abroad were given long lists of items to obtain. Soviet students suddenly discovered new subsidies that were only available when they subscribed to aeronautical magazines. Others received cash when they sifted through newspapers for relevant news, features, interviews and pictures. All the information would be sent to Russia for collation by a vast army of workers. Anything that could help the supersonic effort was handed over to the Tupolev team.

Some initial attempts at spying were absurdly unsubtle. A Romanian diplomat dropped by the London offices of Rolls-Royce, asking for publicity films and photos of the development process. He was politely shown the door.

Posing as a journalist, another agent blew his cover story at Rolls-Royce's Bristol plant by shooting off a barrage of highly technical questions about Concorde's most sensitive engine features.

British and French designers were also invited on expenses-paid lecture tours to the Soviet Union – the KGB hoped to extract information face to face or through wiretaps.

None of these ploys proved particularly productive.

And then one day in January 1965, the front page headline of Britain's *Daily Mail* screamed: "Concorde Spy Alert". Two Britons working for Kodak had been caught passing on information. As the spy claims reached the public's attention, security around the engineering plants was finally stepped up.

But a huge amount of detailed data was already being transferred from France to Russia by a certain Jean Paul Soupert. Soupert was a Swiss chemical engineer. His profession was quite ordinary – but his frequent travel around Europe attracted the attention of the Belgian secret service, who quickly became suspicious. A warning was passed to the French who arrested him with two others. It turned out his colleagues were masquerading as Czech priests at a Catholic school near Toulouse – and had been preparing to penetrate and burgle the Concorde assembly hall.

Soupert had already smuggled out many supersonic secrets. His preferred method of delivery was 35mm film – hidden in toothpaste tubes. Information was sent to East Germany's Stasi secret service in Berlin, by depositing it in the first-class toilet of the Ostend to Warsaw Express. Once captured, Soupert was forced to play a double-agent role. False technical data was passed on to the Soviets in an attempt to confuse them.

⌒∽⌒

The French intelligence agency searched for other spies. On their shortlist of suspects was the head of the Aeroflot office in Paris, Sergei Pavlov. The job was perfect cover – it even enabled him to approach the aeroplane manufacturers.

It turned out that Pavlov had already established a friendship with an employee who worked at an airfield. Not just any airfield, but the very one where trials were being conducted on Concorde's tyres. Pavlov casually requested some tyre scrapings from the runway. But he was now being tailed by the secret service, who finally had the proof that Pavlov was a spy.

The airport worker was asked to pass on a fake tyre sample, made out of something that resembled bubble gum. This outrageous substitute was quickly sent off to Soviet engineers by Pavlov for frenzied analysis. The Soviets must have puzzled over the results for weeks, perhaps even trying to make a tyre out of the soft stretchy substance.

One day Pavlov was at lunch in a popular Paris café when his appointment was suddenly cut short. The streets outside had been blocked and the intelligence services strolled in to arrest their man. He had not come empty handed to the meeting - in his briefcase were the blueprints for Concorde's landing gear. Pavlov had clearly been a busy man - Tupolev's team already had a lot to thank him for.

❧

Aside from the spy networks, information was collected from some direct sources.

On an official trip to Toulouse, Tupelov's son Alexei was given a tour by the plant's director, Bernard Dufour. Alexei was the rising star of Soviet aviation and he quickly noticed a disparity between the engine nacelles on a prototype and the stolen drawings he had in Moscow.

With no warning whatsoever he suddenly whipped out a tape measure which was concealed in a key ring, reached up to make some measurements and smiled. Before Dufour even knew what was happening, Alexei had identified details of a major change in design. "I have measured your engine air-intake," he said politely, "and I find you have increased it by 8%."

❧

There is no doubt that much information was successfully stolen from the Concorde project, but it was often incomplete or out of date. Even when recent plans or drawings were obtained, these were difficult to decipher, being covered in Western annotations unfamiliar to the Soviet designers.

As time went on the British and French governments decided that the leaks had been successfully halted. The manufacturers breathed a collective sigh of relief and got on with their research and development. Unknown to them, the Kremlin's best source would successfully remain undercover for fifteen years. Sergei Fabiew was only exposed when a Soviet defector mentioned his name in 1977.

On being arrested, he cooperated fully, allowing the French to read the secret messages sent to and from Moscow throughout his KGB career. Among the mass of information, they found a glowing note of congratulation. Moscow had been grateful - Fabiew had sent them the entire blueprints for the Concorde prototype.

⁓⁓⁓

The KGB's efforts delighted Tupolev. He was not going to copy Concorde outright, but the data saved time and proved a great reassurance. Groundwork was covered quickly and the Tupolev team were able to rush into a design phase years earlier than planned. As they headed for this final furlong, in 1968, they realised they were now more or less on a level footing with Concorde, and so the KGB was given a new task. Tupolev wanted to know when Concorde would make its maiden flight. He had to be first.

Word finally came through that the Anglo-French venture was scheduled to make its first voyage at the beginning of 1969. It was much earlier than the Soviets had anticipated. But having come this far there was no chance that Andrei was going to take second place. Pressure from Khruschev soon reinforced his determination.

So corners were cut. Unlike Concorde's Olympus engines, which had been tested for months on a converted Vulcan bomber, the new Kusnetsov turbofan engines – which had been developed especially for the TU-144 – would not be flight-tested. The Kusnetsovs would simply be attached to the TU-144 and the plane flown. Statistically, the risks were very high – but so were the stakes.

The workers prepared for the test flight day and night – and finally on New Year's Eve 1968, the Tupolev 144 was rolled out of its hangar at Zhukovsky airfield, near Moscow.

Even now, the cloak of secrecy remained. If anything went wrong, the accident would be quietly brushed under the carpet. So the only people allowed to watch that day were Andrei Tupolev, his son Alexei – and a few key technicians and engineers.

The Moscow air was cold and bitter, but this posed no problem for the four Kustnetsov engines as initial taxiing and brake tests were carried out. At the controls was Edward Vagonovich Elyan, a Russian test pilot hero. Andrei shook his hand and wished him good luck. He was going to need it – this was a very dangerous assignment. On board, an equally experienced flight crew awaited their first take-off attempt.

When fully satisfied with the plane's ground handling, Elyan took the plane out to the end of the runway, turned around and fired up the engines. The plane lurched forwards, gathered speed and finally achieved its first successful take-off. Three low passes were made over the airfield, to the cheers of those below. Half an hour later the small huddle of satisfied engineers greeted the crew with hearty congratulations.

The Russians had done it. They had beaten Concorde into the sky. The Soviet Union now owned the world's first supersonic airliner. In the following weeks, the TU-144 proved its supersonic credentials by travelling through the air at twice the speed of sound.

The Communist propaganda machine went into overdrive. Pictures were pumped around the world. In Moscow, the pages of *Pravda* were overflowing with stories of the TU-144, the editorials revelling in the Communist victory.

The TU-144 had certainly taken the West by surprise. Concorde's planners had completely dismissed the Tupolev, believing it had no chance whatsoever of getting airborne that year. They had underestimated Andrei's determination.

∽◡∾

The European press wasted no time. They reported the plane's striking similarity to Concorde and the new airliner was quickly dubbed "Concordski". Accusations flew between the British and French governments, press and manufacturers. The newspapers asked if the Concorde blueprints had been stolen. But Concorde's designers steadfastly maintained there were only a few similarities. Not everyone was so sure.

Indeed, the TU-144 had many things in common with Concorde. It shared the delta wings and also carried its four engines in nacelles under them. It used a droop nose to aid cockpit visibility on landing and takeoff. It was also tailless. It even used the same nacelle ramp technology developed for Concorde, which controlled the airflow entering the engines.

But the trained eye could also spot key differences. The wing of Concordski was actually quite different to that of its western counterpart. Concorde's shape was totally new, a variant on a classic slender delta with favourable low-speed characteristics. It was carefully sculpted as a result of repeated testing. The design team had eked out every ounce of natural lift they could without compromising the plane's supersonic performance. The Russian wings were simplistic by comparison - the lack of detailing meant the plane would never be efficient at low speeds.

The other big difference was the engines. Concorde had the Olympus turbojet, the trump card that had sealed the signing of the Anglo-French agreement. The Soviet engines were years behind. The USSR had only entered jet engine development after a wartime agreement with Britain, which had given them a

Rolls-Royce Nene engine to copy. Russian engines were an evolution of this now ancient design.

To make matters worse, the Communists still followed Stalin's view that computers were a non-Marxist science. The lack of computers left Soviet engineers lagging behind. The Russians had tried to spy on the Olympus engine, but penetrating the Bristol plant proved more difficult than they had anticipated. More than any other aspect of Concorde, the Olympus engine had been the Holy Grail for the KGB - but the espionage efforts had failed to deliver.

Without the Rolls-Royce blueprints, Tupolev had little hope of achieving the much-needed transatlantic range required to make an SST work. To beat Concorde into the air, he had settled for engines that were unsuited to the supersonic operation. The Russian turbofan engines were in some ways more modern and difficult to build than a traditional jet engine, but they were completely inefficient at supersonic cruise speeds. By choosing the wrong technology, the potential range of the TU-144 was significantly reduced - it also led to appalling inefficiency.

In addition, the TU-144 prototype had its four engines grouped closely together in one pod under the fuselage. Should one engine catch fire, the design introduced the unnecessary risk of it spreading to the remaining three.

Of course, Andrei realised there was much more work to do before this airliner could go into production. The determination to get it into the air first had rushed crucial stages of development.

His aeroplane had been designed to perform just one important task - to win the supersonic race for Khruschev.

Chapter 5

Boom time

... or supersonic fiasco?

The date was March 2, 1969. For two days, hundreds of journalists and onlookers had waited patiently in Toulouse for the weather to clear, for Concorde to finally be given the opportunity to follow the Russians' Concordski into the sky.

Increasingly, the people of France saw Concorde as a wholly French invention, conveniently forgetting the British input.

In some ways, this was not at all surprising. The prototypes had been first wheeled out in France to the sound of the French national anthem. The first flight was to take place in France. And after years of indecision the British had even agreed that Concorde be spelt with an "e", ending a dispute that had lasted a decade. Tony Benn, technology minister at the time, had justified the use of the French spelling by claiming: "E stands for Excellence, for England, for Europe and for Entente Cordiale."

Nevertheless, all the top British executives were in Toulouse that day, hoping as much as their French counterparts that the millions of aeronautical calculations had been done correctly. Today, finally, they would found out whether Concorde could really fly.

After lunchtime, André Turcat, Sud Aviation's test pilot, was asked to prepare for a take-off attempt. He was a little nervous at the prospect, but this was the moment he had been waiting for.

It would make a change from months of performing uninspiring taxiing trips up and down the airfield.

Turcat took the Concorde prototype to the end of the runway, turned the aircraft around and awaited further instructions. Finally, the go-ahead came.

The Olympus engines thundered into action and the prototype started to accelerate down the runway. And then, quite suddenly, the nosewheel rose from the ground for the first time. Concorde was airborne.

Turcat's maiden flight never got anywhere near supersonic speeds. But for the thousands of engineers who had been working on her for a decade, the flight represented the coming of age of their supersonic dream.

After 27 minutes, Turcat brought Concorde 001 down to land and in so doing became a new national hero. Henri Ziegler, president of Sud, Sir George Edwards of BAC and Brian Turbshaw, BAC's test pilot, were the first to greet him and his crew.

The pilot was pleased to inform everyone: "It flies pretty well... as perfect as we had expected."

For all involved, it was a moving moment. The bureaucratic wrangling was forgotten and Britain's attempts to cancel the project now firmly swept under the carpet. In place of the painful disputes that had plagued the project was a cheerful solidarity of purpose. For a few brief moments, all involved could afford to forget the work still required to make Concorde a commercial success. Champagne flowed.

Within months, many parts of France were sporting Concorde supermarkets, Concorde cafés and Concorde bakeries. Citizens found themselves washing their hair with Concorde-branded shampoo and lit their Gitanes with newly manufactured Concorde matches. The entire French nation had seemingly become passionate, enthusiastic and perhaps somewhat over-optimistic supporters of the supersonic project.

∾◦∽

On the other side of the channel, the Brits were a little more divided.

National newspaper advertisements from a newly established "Anti-Concorde Project" were proposing Concorde be cancelled with immediate effect.

The action group revelled in disclosures of spiralling costs and depressing programme delays. They also complained that the supersonic craft would be louder than any competing jet at both take-off and landing. And most critically, the protestors warned of the possible dangers and annoyances of the sonic boom.

Every aircraft that flies supersonically creates a "Bang Sonique" (as the French call it). Its basic characteristics were well recognised before the Concorde project even began. But the Anglo-French manufacturers had decided to ignore the issue, assuming that the effect on those on the ground would be minimal. After all, the plane would be nine miles up in the sky and it was felt that the boom would be hardly noticeable, perhaps sounding like distant thunder. Initial test results from the US supersonic programme seemed to back this theory up.

But it didn't take the British government long to start worrying about the potential complaints. The new British Aviation Minister, Frederick Corfield, was charged with undertaking some research.

What resulted on Tuesday September 1, 1970 was reminiscent of a "Carry On" film. Concorde was to fly down an 800-mile supersonic corridor from Oban in Scotland to a remote part of Cornwall in south-west England. It was the first of 50 planned supersonic tests.

Buildings along the route were rigged up to identify how they would react to the sonic boom. Large blocks of flats were carefully watched. The cathedrals of St David's in South Wales and Truro in Cornwall were both monitored, as was the medieval splendour of Salisbury Cathedral.

The day itself was clearly going to be a great jamboree for Britain's media. All along the route, hundreds of TV cameras, sound recordists and press photographers littered the streets, awaiting their first sonic boom.

It wasn't to be the most remarkable of demonstrations, mainly because test pilot Trubshaw flew 15 miles off course. The journalists were incensed, having spent days planning their coverage. *The Sun* newspaper gladly reported "Ooops, Concorde off course shock", and many broadsheet journalists wondered out loud whether the wrong course had been selected on purpose to minimise the number of negative stories.

As the series of tests continued, the civil servants responsible demonstrated their ability to run a grossly inefficient operation – and one that probably did more harm for Concorde than good.

From the start, the government had promised to give the public warnings before each test, but these promises were often forgotten. In addition, the plane was usually either early or late, meaning monitoring equipment was turned off when Concorde actually flew over. Many tests had to be repeated because of the bureaucratic incompetence. But the tests did prove one thing – the sonic boom had the potential to cause political damage. There were many complaints.

Inevitably, thousands of citizens saw the tests as an opportunity to make a quick buck. Demands for compensation reached the Ministry every day. Cracked ceilings and windows were a frequent complaint, and almost impossible to verify. A group of mink farmers made a claim that their minks were eating each other because of the Sonic Boom.

As it became obvious that the Ministry generally paid up, one Scottish couple decided to make an enormous compensation claim, stating they had had a baby due to Concorde interfering with the "rhythm method" of contraception.

And in Belfast Concorde's first supersonic over-flight led to a bomb scare that gripped the entire city.

Of course, buildings weren't actually being flattened. But the public was altogether unimpressed, and slowly but surely it became obvious that supersonic travel would probably be restricted to the sea. But prohibiting overland supersonic flight limited Concorde's potential routes – and ultimately damaged its commercial viability.

～ ∞ ～

To the excitement of many, both the Concorde and Tupolev manufacturers announced they would be making appearances at the Paris air show of 1971. The battle of the SSTs would be brought out into the open for the first time. Concorde prototypes had already been shown to an excited public – but here was an opportunity to see the planes side by side.

The welcoming atmosphere offered by the Anglo-French consortium – who even removed test equipment to enable visitors to board – was in sharp contrast to the Russian offering. For the entire show, the TU-144 was surrounded by armed guards. Neither the press nor public were allowed a glimpse at its secret interior.

However, one of the Concorde development team did manage to get inside. He would later tell his colleagues that the pilot's seat didn't even have a mechanism for adjustment, suggesting it was designed for just one pilot. Concorde in comparison had a fully electric seat-control mechanism, a real marvel in those days.

Everyone could tell that the Concordski had been rushed into testing. Up close, the corners that had been cut to get her flying were clearly visible. The plane was already showing heavy wear and tear – even though the prototype had flown for a total of just 100 hours. It also sported haphazard modifications and additions that looked decidedly experimental.

The Anglo-French consortium was relieved. The new competitor was nowhere near as refined as Concorde and showed little promise of becoming an effective commercial offering.

～ ∞ ～

The Russians were under no illusions. The data from flight tests showed terrible fuel consumption. The range was so limited that it was hardly worth taking off. In its current state, the TU-144 was next to useless.

The Russians resolved to tackle the problem themselves - this time with their own resources. Reliance on the KGB had helped them progress quickly, and without espionage it would certainly not have been possible to beat Concorde into the skies. But now it was time to turn the TU-144 into a genuinely innovative Soviet SST, one that could beat Concorde on its own terms.

Andrei and Alexei Tupolev returned to Moscow and set to work.

～∽⌐

For the politicians, businessmen and airline chiefs who had received it, the invitation had been compelling - an opportunity to see Concorde in the flesh at the luxurious Air France building, courtesy of *Time* magazine.

Time boss Henry Luce III welcomed guests to what was to be a glorious French luncheon, during which he proceeded to lavish every compliment he could think of on the Anglo-French venture. Concorde symbolized "the future and what it implies for the spectrum of that future, which we trust will be broad and varied and brightly coloured."

For the Concorde chiefs there was every indication this was going to be a fantastic afternoon, soon to be filled with the sound of chinking glasses and happy conversations over the caviar.

But it wasn't to be. Najeeb Halaby, the president of Pan Am, was to give everyone there a rude awakening. Revealing his love of the new Boeing 747 jumbo, with its low running costs, massive capacity and unprecedented range, he suggested to the assembled masses that the Concorde project might not go according to plan after all. After some polite statements about the efforts of the "gallant Gauls and brave British..." who had put together "one of the most fabulous stories of forced technological growth in the history of technology", the American guest revealed he had significant doubts.

The plane's lack of scale meant it could carry just over a hundred people compared to almost four hundred in the 747. Operating costs and maintenance expenses were another worry.

And then in his concluding remarks he dropped a bombshell. The plane, he said, should be shelved. It should be re-developed into a larger aeroplane that could meet the economic demands of higher fuel prices. Halaby proposed the Anglo-French team go back to the drawing board and focus on a new "Super Concorde".

The audience was astonished. Pan Am had been the first airline in the world to seek an option to buy Concorde. And here was the company's boss telling everyone that the beautiful bird in front of them was a dead duck.

Chapter 6

Concordski returns

… and the first French cover-up

Air shows have been around for as long as aircraft. In the early days, they were more circus than trade show. Stunned crowds watched brave men in dangerous flying machines that had to be seen to be believed. With time it became possible to make money from aircraft production - and the purpose of the events changed. The crowds were still there to be dazzled, but now the primary goal was to attract the men in suits and their order books.

The Soviets had had a rough time at the Paris air show of 1971. Their TU-144 SST may have been the first supersonic in the sky - but it was clear to all present that it was a poor imitation of Concorde. The Communist leadership was resolved. Next time round their supersonic must steal the show. Concorde had to be beaten. The Tupolev company must redesign their offering.

For months, Andrei Tupolev and his son Alexei worked non-stop to redesign the plane, desperate to realise their supersonic ambitions.

And then in December 1972, Andrei, the founder of the Russian aerospace industry, died at the age of 84. He had lived just long enough to see his most sophisticated plane reborn - an improved design was rolling off the production lines in Voronezh. But it would now be down to his son to ensure its commercial success.

Alexei Tupolev had been groomed by his father to succeed him since birth - he was already a respected aerospace designer in his own right.

Alexei decided it was time for a re-match. He relished the idea of returning to the Paris air show to steal some of Concorde's thunder.

They chose to go in 1973. It would be an important trip. Few Tupolev airliners were sold outside the Communist bloc. But a supersonic aeroplane was a different matter - perhaps the TU-144 could bring orders and much needed foreign currency into the Soviet Union. Chief pilot Mikhail Kozlov and the TU-144 would have a simple task - to put on such a show that the world would take notice. Russia would prove it had the best supersonic - every airline would want one.

∽ა◡ɾ∾

This was the thirtieth Salon Aeronautique and it was set to be one of the best. The highlight would undoubtedly be the heavyweight title fight: Concorde vs Concordski 2.

Very few people had seen the new TU-144 before it landed in Paris. Visitors were shocked. Western analysts had underestimated Soviet ingenuity once again. She was a bold new design and clearly a threat to Anglo-French ambitions. The new version had gone upscale in every dimension. The plane was longer, its span wider and the cabin larger. Its engines had been moved onto the wings, like Concorde's. But there the similarities between the planes ended. In many ways, this was a wholly new aeroplane. Unlike the earlier prototype, she owed very little to Concorde.

140 passengers could now be carried comfortably, compared to a cramped maximum of 128 on Concorde. Reportedly the plane could fly at Mach 2.4, compared to Concorde's 2.0. Alexei Tupolev told the press he looked forward to flying from Moscow to New York in just three and a half hours. The young designer also claimed his entry was

cleaner and quieter, a good message given the rising influence of the environmental lobby.

One novel innovation was the introduction of small retractable canards behind the cockpit. These short stumpy wings could be brought out at slow speeds to assist in the stability of the plane. Apparently, they also supplied a remarkable 20% more lift. This and many other innovations were new and entirely Soviet designed.

This time it was the Western manufacturers who wanted to copy the Russians.

The experts agreed that the retractable canards were revolutionary, a feature that might well be worth stealing, if not for a Mark II Concorde, then perhaps for an upcoming military project.

∽०౭∽

On the last day of the show, a crowd of 300,000 gathered to see the battle of the supersonics.

Concorde flew first above an excited home crowd. The crew of the TU-144 watched the display from their own aeroplane. It was impressive enough, although the cheers of the crowd were quickly drowned out by the passing roar of the four Olympus engines on reheat. Kozlov felt sure he could do better.

He taxiied the plane up ready for takeoff, thinking through the moves in his mind. His flight had been carefully rehearsed before arriving in Paris. After all, his aeronautical display would be the key to the plane's success.

There were six crew on board the TU-144 that day, all Russian. Just before the flight Michel Tauriac, a French TV journalist, had also tried to talk himself onto the plane. He had been politely refused entry - but Tupolev's chief engineer, Benderov, had agreed to take a TV camera on board and take some footage.

∽०౭∽

Pilots love the freedom and security they enjoy at an air show - the airspace is theirs exclusively. Kozlov had been looking forward to this moment for months. Putting the new supersonic wonder through its paces in front of hundreds of thousands of people would be quite a feat.

But just as he taxiied the plane to the end of the runway, the Russian pilot received a nasty shock. The control tower informed him that his slot time had suddenly been halved. No reason was given, but he would have to comply. Perhaps the French organisers wanted to put a spanner in the works?

This change of plan added to the pressure, but Kozlov was not the kind of person to be easily intimidated.

∽∿⌒

He pushed open the throttles and with that the TU-144's engines roared into action. Everyone agreed it was an impressive take-off, and Kozlov quickly took "Concordski" on a rapid 360-degree turn above the runway. The crowd watched with awe as the crew coaxed every inch of performance from the NK-144 engines. To show off the capabilities of the plane's unique canards, he flew with them extended, demonstrating excellent stability at slow speeds.

On the ground, all the experts were of the same view. It was a superb display. Even the Concorde team could not help but be impressed.

But after a few more tricks, the time-strapped Russians realised they had to return to terra firma.

∽∿⌒

Despite the sunshine, the crew were suffering from very poor visibility. The Russians had decided to fly with the nose up to show the crowd the sleeker lines of supersonic cruise. It wasn't a huge problem in itself but it meant it was much more difficult for Kuzlov to see the runway when trying to land. As he headed towards the ground he suddenly realised he had made a terrible mistake - he was about to land on the wrong runway.

Not wishing to look like an idiot he abandoned the attempt and lit the four reheats, going up into a steep and impressive climb. Up and up Concordski went. Kuzlov soon gained some 3,500 feet. He needed to make this manoeuvre quickly - he didn't have much time left.

∽∾⌒∾

An air show puts great demands on pilots. It is a matter of courtesy as well as safety that they are given the rights to the sky around. Pilots should always be informed of any potential traffic in the area, however unlikely.

So as Kozlov was nearing 4,000 feet he was astounded to see a high-speed jet aircraft in his path. Whether it was moving towards him or away he wasn't quite sure - but if he wasn't careful there might be a deadly collision.

The plane was actually a French Mirage III fighter, which had been flying in the vicinity of the air display with a simple mission: to watch and possibly photograph the new Russian supersonic airliner. The military jet had been there when Concorde flew too, but the French crew had been warned of the danger.

Kozlov had to take quick evasive action. He pushed the nose right forwards into a dive. His action prevented the collision, but a rapid change of course was dangerous - extremely dangerous.

John Farley and Andy Jones, two British pilots who were watching the display take up the story. "This thing was just going up... and then suddenly it just very abruptly levelled off. I mean really violently."

Kozlov had a serious problem. The sudden change in course had disturbed the operation of his NK-144 jet engines. His engines had flamed out, leaving the plane without power.

His only one chance of survival now was to get the engines restarted - and the only way to do that was a sudden steep descent.

Some described the dive as close to vertical. The crowd looked on in wonder. Was this a surprise manoeuvre to end the display and ensure that the Soviets stole the show?

Kozlov's plane came lower and lower as he prayed for the engines to restart. The Russian crew were heading nose-down at speed - the ground filled the entire view in the Tupolev cockpit. Trees and houses were all the pilot and co-pilot could see - and they were growing ever larger in size. He slowly tried to pull out of the dive. What he longed for now was a glimpse of blue sky at the top of the windshield.

The TU-144 strained as it was forced to work harder than it had ever done before. The spars through the wings came under more and more pressure as Kozlov pulled back even further on the controls. He was demanding even more lift from the wing. He knew that the aircraft could get overstressed and that there was a real risk of break-up mid-air. But he had no choice.

The crowd was bemused. Many continued to cheer in anticipation of the next startling stunt. Others stood still, wondering. Just how did this all fit into the planned demonstration?

At about 1,500 feet, just as the plane looked as if it would recover, the right wing suddenly gave in to the stress. The craft flipped over onto its back as the wing detached. The fuselage broke into several pieces and fell from the sky.

Unfortunately for all those aboard, the airframe hadn't been able to handle the strain placed upon it.

∽◡∾

Below the TU-144 was the village of Goussainville. Without warning 150 tonnes of aircraft and fuel suddenly fell from the sky. The six Soviet crew members were killed, as were eight French citizens on the ground, including some children. Sixty others were injured by debris. Fourteen buildings, including the village school, were completely destroyed.

WAAF personnel repairing an RAF Spitfire during The Battle of Britain.
© Hulton-Deutsch Collection/Corbis

Early photograph of Frank Whittle (right) showing off his jet engine invention to journalist Clifford Troke.
© Hulton-Deutsch Collection/Corbis

May 2, 1952. Passengers board the first ever jet-powered passenger flight. Comet G-ALYP (or Yoke Peter) made a successful trip from London to Johannesburg but was destined to crash just nineteen months later, with the loss of all 29 souls aboard.
© Hulton-Deutsch Collection/CORBIS

Dare-devil Captain Charles Yaeger proudly stands beside his Bell X-1 aeroplane, the world's first supersonic aircraft.
© Bettmann/CORBIS

Brian Trubshaw (left) and co-pilot in the cockpit of the British Concorde prototype just prior to the first British flight.
© Hulton-Deutsch Collection/CORBIS

Early British production Concordes being manufactured, following successful testing of prototypes.
© Christian Julius

A Russian TU-144 aircraft receives a well-orchestrated Communist welcome in Kazakhstan.

Concorde in New York in 1977
© Dubois Philippe/Corbis Sygma

British Airways G–BOAE taking off…
© Gordon Roxburgh

… and landing.

The BA fleet was famous for thrilling the crowds on major state occasions.

British Airways BA001 supersonic service to New York takes off from London Heathrow with afterburners alight.
© Johnathan Safford

The final landing and taxi of Air France Concorde F–BVFC at Toulouse, France.
© Gordon Roxburgh

The nose of the now–retired Air France Concorde F-BTSD.
© Gordon Roxburgh

A rare picture of a BA Concorde being towed whilst another lands.
© Gordon Roxburgh

Some of Jetinda Sira's collection of Concorde photographs, taken in the closing months of commercial services.
© Jetinda Sira

BA002 landing at London Heathrow on August 19th, 2003.
© Johnathan Safford.

BA Flight attendant Martine Bell on BA097, a subsonic ferry flight from Toronto to JFK on October 2nd, 2003. She had served Concorde passengers for over 22 years. After landing, a customer approached her to autograph his Concorde book. She gladly took the book, and started to flip through it before exclaiming, "Oh my! That's me!" Sure enough, it was her from many years earlier – posing in front of Concorde.
© Johnathan Safford.

British Airways G-BOAE leaving the British Airways hangar maintenance area…
© Ian Kirby

… another taking off with afterburners alight
© Damien Burke/www.handmadebymachine.com

The view out of the window from seat 23D on BA002 from New York to London Heathrow, 21 August 2003. The aeroplane was flying at Mach 2 at some 57,000ft.
© Johnathan Safford.

G-BOAD's final flight to retirement in New York.

London Heathrow's fire crews give BA Concorde G-BOAG a well deserved send-off. Farewell Concorde.

Soviet officials quickly arrived at the scene by helicopter to find souvenir hunters taking pieces of the wreckage. The destruction covered a wide area, partly because the break-up had taken place in the air. A fuel tank sat in the rafters of a cottage, an engine was left straddled behind some back gardens. A tree was decorated with leaflets in English speaking of the TU-144's comfortable cabin.

This was the first blood spilt on French soil from an aircraft display. The townspeople of Goussainville and the French nation would demand answers.

∾ↄ∽

According to international law, it fell to the French to investigate the incident, but the Soviets weren't happy. Moscow claimed familiarity with the airframe was critical to an investigation and requested an all-Soviet inquiry. Under a compromise deal, a joint commission was established under a French president, with most of the investigative work being done by the military.

Between July and October 1973 the experts sifted the wreckage looking for answers. An official report was eventually completed but never published. Instead, a statement claimed the cause could never be established. This joint press release added that neither a cockpit voice recorder (CVR) nor flight data recorder (FDR) had been recovered intact.

This was a startling claim. Aircraft hull losses run into the thousands, yet only 23 black boxes have ever been destroyed. Every make of CVR or FDR is designed to be crash and fire resistant. In tests they are fired out of air cannons into concrete at hundreds of miles an hour. They are built to last.

Over the last three decades, 145 Tupolev planes have crashed at a cost of over 5,000 lives. But in all these incidents not a single black box was ever destroyed - except in Paris. So how on earth were both the CVR and FDR lost? The crash fire was not even that intense - and most wreckage was distributed away from the flames. The chances that both black boxes were destroyed were almost nil.

Peter Baker, a Concorde test pilot who witnessed the accident, also heard rumours after the accident that the black boxes had in fact been recovered - but that the Russians had claimed they failed to record anything.

Even if they had been lost, the remaining wreckage should have been sufficient to establish the cause. The dying moments of the TU-144 were captured by dozens of TV cameras and seen by some 300,000 eyewitnesses, some of whom happened to be la crème de la crème of the aerospace industry.

For the commission to conclude that they had "no idea" why the crash took place was extraordinary.

One theory informally proposed by the investigation team was that Tauriac's TV camera had caused the crash. The idea was that it was thrown out of the co-pilot's hands and became lodged at the bottom of the control column, wedging the stick fully forwards.

This bizarre tale simply didn't wash. As Kozlov was taxiing out for the most important display of his career, with the entire Kremlin demanding results, it seemed unlikely he would have allowed his first officer to spend the flight making a home movie. The co-pilot's help would have been essential, especially as a new display needed to be improvised. There were four other crew on board and there can be no doubt someone other than the co-pilot would have been doing the filming - if indeed any took place at all.

⌒◡⌒

To this day, French authorities remain cagey when speaking about the incident. In a recent email from the BEA, the French air accident body, Alain Guilldou, head of public affairs claimed, "As usual when a prototype aircraft happens to crash, the civil authority is not in charge of the investigation."

The French authorities never quite got their story straight. The TU-144 was not a prototype - it was a production model straight off the manufacturing line. Nor would this make any difference to the BEA's authority over the investigation. So why was the report deemed unfit for public reading?

❦

In short, the French weren't keen to get the blame for the deaths and the Soviets didn't want their new TU-144 or its engines to receive criticism in a French report. A whitewash worked well for both parties.

It was not for years that the presence of the Mirage III fighter was even confirmed. When it was mentioned on TV to Jean Forestier, an official from the investigative team, he stormed out of the television studio. But André Turcat, who first flew the Concorde prototype, would eventually confirm the "sudden proximity" of a Mirage in the TU-144's flight path, indicated by radar printouts he had seen.

Of course, it is unlikely that the crash would ever have happened if the French had not reduced the TU-144's demonstration time minutes before the demonstration was about to begin - or if the Mirage III fighter hadn't been there in the first place.

Years later, Alexei Tupolev was asked whether the truth had been concealed. He replied slyly: "Commissions, by their very nature, always fail to produce the true picture."

❦

Soviet pride took a terrible pounding following that day in June 1973. It also introduced fears among the public that the supersonics were unsafe - as well as being a potential environmental liability.

But the Tupolev company picked up the pieces. Visits scheduled before the crash went ahead as planned. Mikhail Mikhailov, deputy director of the Ministry of Aviation Production, indicated that the Soviet national airline Aeroflot had placed an order for 30 TU-144s with total orders anticipated between 60 and 75. Internal Soviet airlines would take on the plane first and demonstrate its viability before they attempted to drum up export orders again.

And despite the crash, Western visitors to Tupolev's factory continued to be impressed. Many new techniques had been developed, including the use of titanium in the airframe, a world first. Technically, the plane was extremely impressive and way ahead of anything shipping from the Concorde factories.

Boris Danilov, editor of *Aviation Week*, wrote after a visit: "There can be no doubt that we witnessed a tremendous high-energy programme, using the most modern methods and materials to produce in quantity what must certainly be the most technically advanced transport being built anywhere in the world today. We believe that any group of Western aircraft engineers... would reach the same conclusion."

∽∘∾

The TU-144 entered Aeroflot service in 1975, initially carrying mail and freight between Moscow and Alma-ata in Kazakhstan at Mach 2.05. This was really a route-proving exercise under another name. Insiders at the Tupolev factory concluded that the airframe was a success, but fuel consumption was a problem. The running costs were huge - and the effective range a concern.

While work continued to improve the engines, Aeroflot announced passenger services were to start on November 1, 1977. As the first passengers were boarding, excited press releases poured out from the Kremlin heralding the start of a new era of passenger travel.

But there had been little time to make the plane passenger-friendly. Westerners flying on the first supersonic services were in for a shock. The raw power of the plane was impressive, but the overwhelming impression was not of supersonic speed but supersonic noise. Music was played over the PA for the whole flight - but no one could hear it because of the roar of the engines outside and the extraordinarily loud air conditioning system. Passengers complained that they could not even hear their neighbouring passengers speaking. Many communicated by writing notes to each other.

This was a far cry from Concorde, where passengers had been known to complain that the quiet, vibration-free Mach 2 flight wasn't "exciting enough".

The Russian plane also desperately needed better engines. Without improved fuel efficiency, international services would be impossible. Even fully loaded with fuel, the TU-144 was not able to make it over the Atlantic. And unlike Concorde, the supersonic cruise was only possible with the reheats kept permanently alight.

Major engine modifications were planned by Tupolev when a second crash suddenly occurred on a test flight. A fire started in an engine and quickly spread to the rest of the airframe. Two were killed, three seriously injured. The Soviets hushed up the news - but it was clear the project was in trouble.

Frustrated by the lack of improvements, rising fuel costs and an overall lack of reliability, Aeroflot suddenly cancelled all services in 1978. No reason was given.

Andrei Tupolev's supersonic dream had finally been grounded.

Chapter 7

Supersonic marvel or
white elephant with wings?
... the Concorde team battle for orders

T he sales literature claimed some 240 Concordes would be
shipped to happy customers by 1978. Initially, prospects
looked good. Pan Am's early interest led many an airline to sign
an option deal. BOAC, the forerunner to BA, demanded eight
options. So did Air France. Ten other airlines also signed on the
dotted line, including Air Canada, American Airlines, Lufthansa
and Qantas. At one point, the Concorde sales team had racked up
a theoretical forward order book of some 74 aeroplanes.

But an option deal was no guarantee of a sale. An airline could
easily justify reserving a place on the production line in return
for a small deposit, if only to make sure it didn't end up at the
end of a long queue.

What the Anglo-French consortium never realised was that
there was much work required to convert an option into a sale.
To get an airline to firmly commit to buying, flying and
maintaining the revolutionary new aircraft was to be a very
difficult task indeed.

༄

Geoffrey Knight was the man chosen to get Pan Am to buy
Concorde. Backed up by six senior colleagues, he was dispatched
to New York, knowing he had a real battle on his hands. The

airline's options expired in a few weeks, whereupon Pan Am would either be placing a firm order or allowing their options to lapse.

It was a difficult time for the American airlines. The introduction of the Boeing 747 would soon double seating capacity on many routes, just as growth in passenger traffic was levelling off. The overall effect on Pan Am was a serious worsening of its financial position. The company's bankers had recently agreed a massive $280 million emergency loan to keep it afloat - but some analysts believed it would go bust anyway.

The bankers seemed to be the key to securing a Concorde order. Knight believed his role was to turn them into enthuisastic supporters - the bankers keeping Pan Am afloat had never been so powerful. So Knight and his team invited hundreds of Pan Am's financiers to a supersonic conference at a New York hotel. The invitations were readily accepted - all the bankers were fully aware of the potential significance of this new supersonic passenger jet.

Knight's trump card in these critical discussions was a controversial survey. According to the statistics provided by a top American market research firm, the business traveller was willing to pay up to 40% more to fly on Concorde. The result, at least according to Knight, was that Pan Am needed Concordes. If it didn't buy them, it would lose its key transatlantic business customers to competitors, particularly the state-owned BOAC and Air France.

The Anglo-French team's strategy was good and simple: to persuade Pan Am's bankers that they had no choice but to proceed. In the evening, the team switched mode to a charm offensive, with a lavish cocktail party hosted by Michael Heseltine, the then British Aviation Minister. He had been given a single task by his Prime Minister - to sell Concorde to the world.

The next day the sales team reviewed events. They all agreed - so far so good. The bankers seemed to be falling into line, so now it was time for direct negotiations with the airline.

They quickly got on the phone and left a message, proposing a meeting. To their surprise there was no response. So they called again and suggested a dinner. The invitation was politely declined.

Pan Am was in no rush to debate the purchase. Apparently, the airline was considering the issue internally, and would let them know in due course. As days went by, the Concorde team found themselves sitting in their hotel rooms, constantly hoping that the telephone would ring. Occasionally they would manage to get an off-the-record meeting with a Pan Am employee, usually in an expensive restaurant. But as the expenses bill soared, progress remained painfully slow.

As decision day approached, the Pan Am order was looking less and less likely. Surely there would be more activity if the order was going to be confirmed? The team had also heard a rumour that their key operating forecasts were being disputed internally at Pan Am. But they had no opportunity to defend themselves - or their numbers.

So the Europeans played their trump card. Concorde's manufacturers announced they would be willing to lease some Concordes to Pan Am, to give them an opportunity to put them to the test. They were also prepared to extend the deadline for a decision by some 90 days.

But this bold and desperate move failed to have any noticeable effect on the airline's enthusiasm. On the evening of January 30, the Concorde taskforce finally discovered that their worst fears had been realised. Pan Am would be turning its back on supersonic services.

Knight left quietly down a discreet service escalator and then out of a side door, carefully avoiding the awaiting press. The rest of the sales team headed for the bar, realising the cancellation was a disaster for the entire Anglo–French enterprise. Pan Am's rejection meant every airline in the world would now be questioning the plane's economics.

~∞~

There was more bad news to come. Environmental protestors would soon be pressuring the US into introducing strict noise regulations at American airports - the new rules allowed a Boeing 747 to fly, but prevented Concorde even landing in New York. And as if that wasn't bad enough, the fear of the sonic boom was making it ever more likely that Concorde would be banned from flying supersonic over US territory.

Back in Europe, the sales team decided that they wouldn't give up. They had been working on the plane for over a decade now, and a few lousy Americans wouldn't be allowed to spoil the party. In a show of determination, it was decided that the Concorde prototypes should fly around the world on a truly global supersonic sales pitch.

With New York officials already refusing landing rights, Texas was the chosen spot for a US tour. The trip nearly ended prematurely when Concorde narrowly avoided a mid-air collision with a light aircraft full of over-zealous press photographers. The supersonic climbed steeply to avoid disaster, just as it was about to land. On the second attempt, Concorde landed safely to an excited welcome from thousands. It seemed the whole state had turned out to see this new supersonic wonder.

"Everyone agrees Concorde's a show stopper", screamed the *Dallas Times Herald*. Hundreds of newsmen from all over the continent were there to record the first supersonic landing in North America. The vast majority of their reports were extremely positive. The Concorde team's morale started to pick up once more.

Supersonic sales trips followed to South America, to Asia, to Japan, and to Australia. Everywhere she flew, she was greeted with enthusiasm, with the exception of a stop-over in Angola. Here the pilot managed to wave the wrong flag out of the cockpit window and in so doing caused a major diplomatic incident as well as a full-scale riot. The British captain had accidentally chosen the flag of the country's rebel insurgents.

Another unexpected incident took place when the sales team targeted the Philippines and its fiery dictator Ferdinand Marcos.

His wife Imelda suggested a supersonic shopping trip to Hong Kong to try out the new aeronautical revolution.

The Concorde team were happy to oblige, failing to realise that the entire plane would be filled with her purchases on the return leg. Not content with this hugely expensive one-day shopping trip, she insisted on repeating the experience the very next day. Sadly, Imelda's enthusiasm for shopping never quite transferred to supersonic aircraft - and the Concorde personnel left the Philippines empty handed.

~~~

In the end, Concorde's marketing trips around the world achieved little.

In North America Air Canada, American, Braniff, Eastern, Pan Am and TWA had all taken out options. Elsewhere there were agreements in place with Air India, Iran Air, JAL, Lufthansa, MEA-Air Liban, Qantas and Sabena.

But every single one of these airlines cancelled their options. The sales teams watched the order book crumble and morale plunged to new depths. Not a single firm order from outside Britain or France would ever be placed.

There were many reasons for this. For a start, the global economy was reeling from oil price increases and Concorde drank an awful lot of fuel compared with conventional aircraft. The Boeing 747 was also swamping the market with unwanted capacity, which the airlines were finding hard to sell. And most critically, the cost of the supersonic plane was simply too high. Fuel, maintenance - even the purchase price - were not attractive.

So the airlines ignored the pleas of the Concorde sales team and focused instead on filling their fleets of subsonic Boeing 747s. The future would be about providing slow but cheap travel.

Even in Britain and France, the national airlines protested when they were finally asked to sign their cheques. British Airways publicly claimed the plane would be loss-making - and insisted on government cash if it was going to run any supersonic services. The airline got its subsidies – and Michael Heseltine got a sales deal for Concorde, the one and only contract he was ever to negotiate.

Air France reluctantly agreed to purchase its share of the planes too, but behind the scenes there was considerable wrangling as to who would end up paying for the resulting losses.

A plan for a model "B" or Mark II version of Concorde with quieter engines and a longer range was quietly dropped, as the British and French governments finally decided that enough was enough. Production would be capped at 16 aircraft, unless more orders suddenly came in from somewhere else. For a few years, the production facilities were preserved in the vain hope that the aerospace market would suddenly change. But sadly for the thousands of workers at Bristol's Filton plant and at Toulouse, the orders never materialised.

The multi-million-pound manufacturing jigs would eventually be sold to scrap metal merchants and melted down.

Meanwhile, a few innovations from the American SST programme did make it into service – the TVs and entertainment systems were introduced on 747s. These simple innovations did more than anything else to ensure time flew by.

⤳✲⤶

It was with some trepidation that Air France and British Airways prepared their Concordes for the start of commercial flights in 1976.

The initial services would be modest, with BA providing a twice-weekly trip from London to Bahrain and Air France a Paris to Rio de Janeiro route via Dakar. The airlines launched these services simultaneously on January 21. Every seat was taken – some of the passengers had booked their tickets twelve years earlier. Huge crowds appeared at London Heathrow and Paris Charles de Gaulle (CDG) airport to watch the inaugural flights.

At 11:40 precisely both pilots fired up their Olympus engines and took off into the skies. Finally, two decades after the project was originally conceived, the first paying passengers were about to experience intercontinental travel at Mach 2.

But for Concorde to succeed commercially the key would be landing rights in the US. Fierce opposition to noise levels meant these attractive transatlantic routes were off limits for now. Behind the scenes, the British and French politicians and diplomats were trying every avenue available to get the Americans to back down. Finally on 4 February, the US Secretary of Transportation William T Coleman gave permission for a 16 month trial period of one Concorde service per day to Washington, and two to New York. Other supersonic services were also launched, including a BA London to Singapore service via Bahrain, which was jointly run with Singapore Airlines.

But in the end only the scheduled flights to New York, a seasonal London to Barbados route and a few charter flights would ever make money consistently.

∽∾∾

On numerous occasions the British and French governments engaged in creative accounting to save their supersonic programme.

In February 1979, Britain's Labour administration was forced to write off the £160 million BA owed for the purchase of the original planes, in return for 80% of future supersonic profits. At the same time it gave BA the keys to the last two British Concordes in production – Air France got access to three more planes at the same time.

As well as cancelling some huge debts, the British and French governments agreed to pay for the huge maintenance costs involved in supporting the aircraft.

When the project was originally envisaged it was assumed that there would be hundreds of Concordes flying the globe. The continuing research and development costs would be shared among a large number of supersonic carriers. But with a maximum of 14 aircraft going into commercial service, the governments had no choice but to stump up for these expensive activities.

One of the most significant costs was a full-sized Concorde replica in Farnborough, which was constantly put through thousands of simulated flight cycles to ensure that the airframe was capable of the longevity envisaged. The cost of this important but massive undertaking ran into millions of pounds every year.

∽∾∽

In May 1979, the British people elected their first female Prime Minister. Margaret Thatcher won her mandate on a policy of free market economics and industrial modernisation. Concorde and BA's finances would not escape her attention.

Sir John King was appointed as the new chairman of British Airways and was informed that the government wanted the airline to be turned around – and privatised – as a matter of urgency.

As the entire organisation was turned upside down the BA board established a supersonic "profit centre", headed by two of its pilots, Captain Brian Walpole and Senior First Officer Jock Lowe. Knowing that Concorde was far from being anything like a centre for profit, the two urgently worked to save the division. They ran around the entire operation identifying potential cost savings as well as opportunities for improved revenues. Slowly the British Concorde fleet limped towards a profit.

But then a new crisis struck. In the spirit of free-market economics, the government decided it would no longer fund the British support costs for Concorde. It unexpectedly asked BA to consider paying for these itself. If the answer was no, the supersonic project would close forthwith, not only in Britain but almost certainly in France too.

The French President Francois Mitterand was thinking along the same lines, and becoming increasingly concerned about the continuing losses. For the first time since the original supersonic treaty, the respective governments were agreeing that spending had to be brought under control. In hushed tones, officials at the Anglo-French summit of 1981 discussed how a Concorde closure might be executed.

But to everyone's surprise, BA responded to the government threats by saying it wanted to negotiate. In so doing, it caused a sea change in the public's perception of Concorde. Here for the first time was the British national carrier claiming Concorde had a viable and profitable future.

A deal was brokered a year or so later. Concorde was saved, at least for now. The new deal meant BA would keep 100% of all future supersonic profits. It would also acquire the remaining spare parts still owned by the government. The very considerable financial burden of manufacturer support and maintenance was to become a BA responsibility, though the Concorde test plane in Farnborough would be an early casualty of cost cutting.

For the government, there was a lump payment of £16.5 million. The UK taxpayer wasn't exactly getting a great return – after almost a billion pounds of expenditure it was about to get about 2% of its investment back. But the deal marked a turning point for Concorde – for the first time, the plane was to be run on pure profit and loss accounting. Luckily for BA, the division quickly became profitable, largely because the business market began to blossom in the mid-1980s. Passenger loads on the transatlantic routes increased year on year.

Eventually, the newly privatised BA was able to bank supersonic profits of around £60 million a year.

Air France didn't have quite as much luck. It lacked a large gateway like London Heathrow from which it could pluck significant numbers of connecting passengers. But the French national airline continued to get government support for its operations, and the French supersonic services survived – at least for now.

By 1987, BA's supersonic fleet had recorded its millionth scheduled transatlantic passenger – and Air France was nearing the 700,000 mark. Thirteen years later, as the millennium drew to a close, BA's total profits from Concorde had reached almost a billion pounds.

The Concorde Experience

Chapter 8

Flying with Celebrities
"I only wish the flight had lasted longer"

Few have met more of the world's rich and famous than Concorde's cabin crew. For thirty years the passenger list to and from New York remained a veritable "Who's Who" of politics, money and showbusiness. Aircraft staff would eagerly await distribution of the passenger list, to see which heroes and heroines they were about to serve - and in some cases flirt with.

Indeed, travelling supersonic almost guaranteed you would meet a celebrity or two. A tired group of business travellers once found themselves singing Beatles songs on a supersonic Christmas flight - with Paul McCartney on guitar.

In 1985, passengers were astonished to see Phil Collins on board when he was supposed to be playing at the Live Aid charity concert at London's Wembley Stadium. He had actually already done his bit - and was flying supersonic to participate in the charity's US concert too. He became the first person to appear on both sides of the Atlantic on the same live TV show.

So what was it really like flying on Concorde?

Check-in was always a pleasure, with passengers able to turn up just thirty minutes before take-off. Of course, there were no queues for those rich enough to fly supersonic. The staff at the dedicated Concorde desks treated their customers like royalty. Sometimes they were.

On passing through fast-track security, you would quickly deposit yourself in the Concorde lounge. It was the height of luxury: acres of expensive leather sofas and designer armchairs. A bar that looked horribly expensive, but where the drinks were free. Staff everywhere politely asking whether "Sir" or "Madam" would like to sample some culinary delights. The complimentary food and drinks were remarkable, reminiscent of a good lunch at the Ritz. There was of course champagne, but it was quite unlike the fare normally served to passengers on other first and business-class flights. Only the very best of vintages would do for the Concorde élite.

Sitting in the lounge had other benefits too - there was always some celeb-spotting to be done. Whilst it was impolite to stare, a sly glance around the place (preferably behind the cover of sunglasses) usually did the trick.

And then the announcement would come. A polite and casual call for what was a unique experience. "We are now boarding the supersonic service to New York." At most airports it was not even necessary to leave the lounge. A special gate had been constructed to ensure you could walk directly from your leather sofa to your leather chair on the plane.

∾◡∾

For those new to Concorde, the cabin was always a shock. It was small, very small.

The head height was surprisingly low - tall passengers had to bend down to even get to their seats. No luxurious flat beds, either, despite the price. Concorde's passengers sat on the most expensive economy-sized seats in the world. There were two pairs on either side of the aisle, guaranteeing either a great view out of the remarkably small window, or a good view up and down the aisle for some more celeb-spotting.

Once everyone was sitting comfortably and carefully strapped in, the pilot would welcome passengers, many of whom were regulars.

It would now be time to experience the legendary Concorde take-off. Concorde was propelled down the runway at nearly twice the speed of any normal plane – thanks to the powerful forces of the Olympus engines on reheat. The acceleration would push you hard against the back of your seat. Looking out of the windows, you would be amazed by the speed built up before the plane finally lifted off the ground.

And then, depending on the airport and runway, the plane would make an almost immediate sharp bank to the left or right at only a few hundred feet. A rapid change of direction was incorporated into take-offs to reduce the noise experienced by local residents. The roar that Concorde left in her wake had always been the subject of sharp criticism. The pilot's task was one of damage limitation.

Once in the air, the first twenty minutes would be spent heading out towards the sea at the slower speeds more normally associated with a 747. Few passengers realised that the steep ticket prices were partly inflated by this most unremarkable stage of the flight. Concorde's sophisticated engines may have been great during an extended supersonic cruise, but they were always horribly inefficient when the plane lumbered along subsonic. At 450mph or so, fuel consumption was grim.

The travelling public generally remained entirely oblivious to the tasks being performed up front in the cockpit, where many additional burdens were put on the crew. To maximise efficiency, the centre of gravity of Concorde had to be moved for different parts of the flight. This was achieved by pumping fuel from tank to tank when required – a unique engineering solution which was unparalleled, and all the more remarkable for a plane of its time.

❧

Once over the sea, Concorde would prepare to go supersonic. Only fishing boats and ocean liners would hear her sonic boom now. The pilot would begin the rapid acceleration into the stratosphere with the legendary reheats being used again until Concorde reached Mach 1.7.

Passengers new to Concorde generally watched the sophisticated cabin displays transfixed, eagerly awaiting the world-breaking speeds. For Concorde's pilots and its regular passengers, this "breaking" of the sound barrier became quite routine. It was all too easy to forget how many test pilots had lost their lives trying to accomplish the very same feat.

Mach 1 would finally be reached and surpassed at around 40,000 feet, Mach 2 at between 50,000 and 60,000 feet. By now, Concorde was flying at twice the height of a conventional plane, shooting past the 747s below at almost three times their speed. Concorde's passengers were travelling faster than the speed of a bullet. Nevertheless, the ride remained smooth and in the cabin they enjoyed the finest cuisine, accompanied by splendid wines.

According to some frequent flyers, the French team had a slight edge on the culinary front, but you were unlikely to complain about the British food either. These weren't normal airline meals – they were a veritable feast.

By the time Concorde reached maximum speed, the view out of the window was quite remarkable. If you looked closely, you could just about see the curvature of the Earth. With a bit of imagination you could almost convince yourself that you were looking down from space. Unless you happened to work for NASA, you were unlikely to get closer.

⌒⌒⌒

In the good old days, as the Concorde crew called them, the pilot would also keep his door ajar so that passengers could take a glance out of the rather small cockpit window.

And certainly, if you were a Concorde pilot and you happened to have a Bill Wyman on board, it was considered traditional to offer him the opportunity to watch the crew in action. Such practices ended after the September 11th tragedy.

As reinforced and locked cockpit doors were installed, cockpit tours ended.

⌒⌒⌒

Whether they were businessmen, musicians, politicians or artists, Concorde regulars always debated one important topic: where to sit. The front portion of the plane was clearly more comfortable. The roar of the engines and resulting vibrations were substantially lower – a seat up front also offered superior views.

So regulars often vied for window seat 1D. Sitting here would mean you were residing in the very same place occupied by the bums of Sir Elton John, Henry Kissinger, Robert Redford, Margaret Thatcher, Mick Jagger, Liz Hurley and Joan Collins.

Interviewer extraordinaire Sir David Frost was an exception to the rule. As one of the most regular supersonic passengers, Sir David came to prefer a window seat on row 23, due to the comparatively sparsely populated rear cabin. With an empty seat next to him, he found it easier to grab a quick nap. Sir David was an enthuisastic Concorde supporter who famously claimed it was the only method by which you could be in two places at the same time.

Queen Elizabeth II and the late Princess Diana may well have not seen eye to eye on everything – but they certainly agreed on one thing. They absolutely loved the same Concorde seat. 1A was the place to be.

Concorde seats 13A, 13B, 13C and 13D were never allocated. In an effort to please superstitious American travellers, the airlines decided to skip row 13 when they originally fitted out the plane.

As for the airplane enthusiasts – who had often saved up for years to try out supersonic flight – they had different objectives. Most preferred the back part of the plane. OK, so the view was obscured by the wing, but here there was a wonderful opportunity to hear the true power of the Olympus engine reheats.

༄༅

Despite its age and performance, pilots said that Concorde was extremely easy to fly.

When the plane was developed computer systems were very basic - IBM was still ten years away from getting a computer to rest on a desk, rather than fill an entire room. Nevertheless, Concorde's specification included the first full fly-by-wire system, so complex that the plane could land itself automatically. It could go all the way down to 15ft above ground before the pilot had to decide whether to proceed with the landing or abort. The specification remained leading edge for decades.

This automatic landing functionality was critical for Concorde, partly because cockpit visibility was so poor, even with the nose down at take-off and landing. It was extraordinarily sophisticated technology for a plane conceived in the 1960s.

༄༅

Eventually it was time to stop drinking the airline's vintage champagne. The tray tables were folded up and the passengers prepared for their Concorde landing. As soon as descent started the speed quickly dropped. The plane headed down towards earth much more rapidly than she had risen: the angle could be quite disconcerting.

But the major worry for Concorde pilots coming into America was the danger presented by private pilots flying in the airspace around New York. Unlike Europe, where a Cessna light aircraft is usually banned from anywhere near a major airport, the US is infested with small planes which are given an extraordinary degree of freedom. On many US landings, the Concorde pilots had to duck and dive to take evasive action as they approached New York's airport. Behind them, the passengers remained oblivious as they fastened their seat belts.

The Concorde landing was an eerie - though exhilarating - sensation. Passengers could sense the aeroplane falling rapidly towards earth, whilst the plane was still pointing steeply upwards. Many commented that it felt like a landing - but looked like a take-off. The back wheels would hit the runway several seconds before the front.

Soon after the loud thud at touchdown, passengers would hear a powerful screech of the carbon brakes and the brief thunder of the engine reverse thrusters - it was always an exciting moment for the enthusiasts at the back of the plane.

Concorde's unusual landing method created problems for photographers too. The plane always looked the same whether it was taking off or landing, leading to many an incorrectly captioned photograph in newspapers and magazines.

❧

Generally, the trip from New York to London or Paris took a little over three hours, about the same duration as many internal European flights. No wonder some executives used Concorde to commute between New York and Europe.

In 1979, BA Captain Jock Lowe became the first pilot to take Concorde across the Atlantic in less than three hours. The world record for London to New York was broken again in 1988, when the trip was made in just 2 hours and 55 minutes. The all time best was 2 hrs 52 minutes and 59 seconds, courtesy of BA's Captain Les Scott and Senior First Officer Tim Orchard.

One well-travelled Concorde passenger, who presumably had enough air miles for several lifetimes, was oil tycoon Fred Finn. By 1992 he had apparently racked up his 700th trip, having spent as much time in the air as many of Concorde's pilots. Whether he got a discount on the full price of $5 million is not known - but he had certainly travelled the equivalent of five return trips to the moon.

Paris Revisited

Chapter 9

The Paris Crash:
Jacques Chirac's lucky day
... and the truth behind the French accident investigation

Jacques Chirac sat in the first-class cabin of the Air France Boeing 747, recovering from the long-haul flight from Tokyo. The President of France had just had a testing time at the G8 summit. In an attempt to justify France's latest global ambitions, he had ended up in heated exchanges with the Americans. They never quite saw eye to eye.

Out of his window, Chirac was pleased to see France's pride and joy, Concorde, waiting for take-off. Wasn't she a fantastic example of French engineering? Occasionally, state trips involved chartering the aeroplane - those flights were always the most memorable.

Chirac and the many other passengers gazed out at Concorde as she started up her engines and then watched, appalled, as a trail of flames suddenly appeared behind her. She lurched from the ground, clearly struggling.

Minutes later, news came in that Concorde had crashed nearby. Nobody could believe what they had just witnessed. A shocked Chirac initially wanted to go straight to the crash site. His advisors restrained him, realising the security escort would hamper the rescuers' efforts.

Chirac probably didn't realise that the Concorde had come extremely close to crashing into the very Boeing 747 in which he had been a passenger. If the two had collided, the death toll would have increased at least four-fold. The French nation would also have been left without a president.

❧

Workers in Air France's HQ had also witnessed the grim sequence of events. As the flames followed the plane down the runway the employees had become glued to the spectacle before them, some even clambering on chairs to get a better view.

When Concorde took to the air, some had breathed a sigh of relief. Others feared the burning plane would be out of the reach of the airport's fire services. For a few minutes it was not easy to tell what was going on - and the workers huddled together, praying for a miracle.

But then the unmistakable sign of tragedy appeared: a mushroom cloud of smoke on the horizon. In the offices, a moment of stunned silence and then cries filled the air. All across the airport, Air France workers tapped into computer terminals to bring up the passenger and crew manifest for flight 4590.

The computer screens told many that they had lost dear friends.

❧

As Chirac left the airport the accident teams were already converging on Air France's offices.

Soon there were government officials from France, Britain and Germany, specialists from British Aerospace and Aerospatiale, engine experts from Rolls-Royce and its French equivalent SNECMA.

Under international law, the French Bureau d'Enquêtes et d'Analyses (BEA) would head up the investigation. A long-standing agreement to share work on Concorde-related incidents meant two senior investigators from the British Air Accident Investigation Branch (AAIB) would join the team. Ever since the Yoke Peter crash investigation in the 1950s, the AAIB had been considered one of the finest air accident investigators in the world and all such help was welcomed by the French, at least initially.

The investigators faced an uphill struggle in their search for the truth. They would have to deal with complex aeronautical technology, specialist operating procedures and thousands of pieces of wreckage: the resulting report could take months or even years to complete.

❧❧❧

The experts were quickly divided up into small teams to examine every aspect of the flight and its preparation. Some were dispatched to search for clues on the runway, others to rake through the crash site. Air traffic control tapes were taken away for review, maintenance records seized.

Alan Simmons of the AAIB investigation unit was one of the first on the runway. It was quite a sight, a long sickening trail of debris left in the wake of Concorde's take-off.

Walking along the tarmac he found a kilometre-long carpet of soot plus what appeared to be skid marks from tyres. The trail began at the centreline – but eventually veered off to the left. Did Concorde run off the side of the runway before she finally got airborne?

The evidence suggested not, but she had clearly been within metres of leaving the runway: a sturdy runway edge light lay obliterated by Concorde's tyres.

If she had ploughed into the grass at high speed, Concorde would have been severely damaged. It is unlikely the undercarriage would have survived the effects of the rough surface. The aeroplane would then have continued on her collision course with the Boeing 747 that lay directly in front of her. Simmons knew it was inconceivable that a high-speed impact between Concorde and a Boeing 747 would have resulted in anything other than a huge number of casualties. A tragedy on this scale would have been comparable with the worst air accident in history, when a KLM jet collided with a Pan Am 747 on the ground in Tenerife in 1978, killing almost six hundred people.

Simmons walked up and down the runway surveying the skid marks, burnt tyre fragments and other debris. The team found a metal strip, which analysis would later show had fallen off a Continental DC-10. The part was found right next to a section of Concorde's second tyre. Also on the runway was a small part of the left-hand wing. It was tiny, about 30cm square, and seemed to have been forced out of the plane.

∞∞

As the evening shift turned up for work at Air France's maintenance depot, everyone was in sombre mood.

The press had already established one key fact. One of Concorde's engines had been undergoing engineering work minutes before take-off. With eyewitness reports of flames coming from an engine, this seemed like the smoking gun. The press believed the repair had been botched. Had the maintenance depot screwed up, and killed 113 people in the process? The ultimate nightmare of every technician and engineer was being played out in the media. Everyone at the depot was holding their breath, waiting for news and hoping for exoneration.

Despite the cramped working conditions and the lingering whiff of aerospace fuel, the mood at an aircraft maintenance facility is normally rather jovial. Not that evening. Tensions were running extremely high and the presence of the top brass didn't help. Normally, only technicians and shift-planners worked this late. But everyone senior in Air France maintenance seemed to be there, right up to the upper management of the long-haul operations directorate. Additional unknown figures, all wearing suits, wandered around with their visitor badges.

∞∞

Some time later, one of the Air France engineers made an alarming discovery. He found a small but important part of a Concorde jet. And however many times he checked the instructions or checklists, he found himself coming to the same conclusion.

The part sitting in front of him in the maintenance hangar shouldn't be there at all. It should have been attached to Concorde F-BTSC when it took off – and therefore, presumably, have been attached to it when it crashed in Gonesse.

A small group of carefully selected French investigators set to work on the missing part but kept the discovery under wraps, at least for the time being.

Sifting through the maintenance records they discovered Concorde F-BTSC had just completed an A01 check, a major operation that had taken five days. There had been one unusual requirement during the procedure – a part replacement on something called the bogie beam.

The bogie beam was a key structural element on the undercarriage leg. The leg had four wheels and retracted into the underside of the fuselage after take-off. The bogie beam connected these wheels to the main leg. It was joined to the leg by a large thick axle, which pegged the two parts together. Two thin rings called shear bushes aligned the axle. Keeping these shear bushes in position was a spacer. The spacer was the part that had been left behind.

Changing the beam was a complicated task, requiring the removal of the undercarriage. Concorde had to be jacked up like a car with a flat tyre.

In 31 years of flying Concorde, Air France had never carried out this procedure before. But the manual was quite clear on how it should be done – and it should have presented no problems. The shear bushes and spacer were to be extracted, using a special tool held in the stores. The manual described this procedure in detail – and also explained how the parts should be put back again afterwards. But none of this had been done properly. The manual had simply not been followed.

This was a clear breach of procedure. The primary rule of modern aircraft maintenance is to take humans out of the decision-making loop. Operations are laid out like the instructions for assembling an Airfix model. The manuals are clear and simple – there is no potential for ambiguity.

And it wasn't just one irresponsible individual: a job of this size would have required a small army of technicians. You don't jack up the wing of a Concorde and leave it in the hands of a single engineer.

ᘒᔠᔢ

In the days after the disaster, news of the deadly metal strip quickly leaked to the press.

Journalists discovered that this sharp object was responsible for the bursting of a tyre, and were told how the tyre then punctured a wing and ultimately caused the fire. Air France's maintenance issues were to escape the full glare of public attention.

ᘒᔠᔢ

As the investigation continued, the AAIB's British accident investigators became worried.

When they were invited to most countries they were treated like royalty. Every piece of evidence was immediately made available. But not in Paris – it was becoming increasingly difficult for the AAIB to do their job at all. Alan Simmons and his team couldn't help feeling they were working in hostile territory.

They were refused access to much of the evidence. "Judicial processes" carried out by judges with no particular expertise in aviation hampered the British investigators at every stage. Time and time again a request for documents would be denied or delayed for weeks. Simple copies of photographs would take over a month to reach them. The French seemed to be trying to keep the AAIB out of the investigation.

And so, when in August 2000 the BEA released the first of three reports on the Concorde crash, the British investigators hadn't even been allowed to see the document properly in advance. The report was the first official word regarding the cause of the crash – and should have been an important milestone in the investigation. But the 63-page document hadn't even been checked properly before publication. Careless rushed errors in calculations and glaring contradictions filled its pages. Totals for fuel levels and weights didn't even add up.

The entire document also directed the reader straight to the same simple conclusion the press had been told to expect: a metal strip burst a tyre; this ruptured the fuel tank causing a fire; the fire made the plane crash. According to the BEA, it was as simple as that.

In addition, this report – and indeed all future reports – made the order of events very difficult to decipher for anyone wanting to carry out their own analysis. The time index of the flight data recorder was recorded as a coded six–digit number rather than a time. The debris and marks on the runway were recorded either by their distance from the runway threshold – or by the number of the concrete slab on which they had been found. The aeroplane's position was sometimes supplied as time – and on other occasions as a time index on the flight data recorder. So for the casual observer, it was very difficult to identify the sequence of events.

This first report also recommended the suspension of Concorde's certificate of airworthiness. With Air France's Concordes still grounded and BA's still flying, only one company was affected by the recommendation. And so it was that on 16 August, a BA Concorde taxiing for take-off to New York was asked to return immediately to the terminal. The pilot brought the white bird back to the gate to find a depressed airline waiting to greet their passengers.

BA's flagship had been taken away.

Concorde probably did need to be grounded, at least until her tyres were sorted out.

As long ago as 14 June 1979, tyre problems had proved to be a major issue for the aircraft. On that particular day, Air France F–BVFC was leaving Washington Dulles airport for Paris when one tyre deflated. The increased load created a domino effect with another adjacent tyre immediately bursting under the additional strain. The wheel rims ended up in contact with the runway at high speed, showering the underside of the wing with shards of metal. The fast moving pieces of metal were heavy enough to puncture the wing.

As a result, the fuel tanks suddenly burst open.

Fortunately, a certain Bill Lightfoot was on board that day. Bill was an aviation consultant and when the plane lifted up on take-off he heard the sudden shuddering and was further alarmed to see something fly past his window at high speed.

Loosening his seatbelt to look through the window, he saw a gaping hole in the wing. It had rough edges of aluminium skin sticking out in odd directions. Something had forced its way through the skin from below. Fuel was starting to flow out – and at an increasingly rapid rate. Fortunately, it had not yet ignited.

He discreetly reported his observations to the steward who claimed Bill was mistaken – everything was, he was told, quite normal. Lightfoot was insistent. A member of the cockpit crew should inspect it immediately, he stated, or he would get out of his seat and go up to the cockpit himself.

Eventually the steward agreed to discuss the issue with the pilot – Bill was making quite a fuss. The co-pilot came down to see him, and was shown where to look. Realising he was about to be ignored again, the passenger forced the co-pilot's head up against the window, now pleading to be taken seriously. The co-pilot's reassurances ceased mid-sentence. Uttering "Mon Dieu", he suddenly went quite pale.

Fortunately for all concerned, the Air France Concorde later touched down safely.

After this incident a number of airworthiness directives were issued, specifying modifications that Concorde would need before she could fly again. Most aircraft receive such directives. Some older types of plane have clocked up hundreds.

This particular directive meant Concorde gained a system to detect under-inflated tyres. Reinforced tyres were also introduced. Designed to cope with twice their normal load, they gave some protection in the event of a failure. The airlines felt this was a satisfactory solution.

Tyre-related incidents became much less frequent after the modifications. But there were still occasional problems and by the time of the tragic Paris crash, BA was changing its Concorde tyres every 25 cycles, far more frequently than the designers had originally envisaged.

But these improved procedures focused on the danger of bursts due to wear and tear or poor maintenance. The danger of an external factor was never fully considered, despite the runway debris often seen by pilots at CDG and JFK airports. What Concorde really needed was a tyre that would be less susceptible to bursting - and less damaging if it did.

Only after the Paris crash would such a change be finally forced on the airlines.

⌒⌒⌒

Continental Airlines was to come under scrutiny in the months following the crash. It owned the plane that dropped the sharp metal strip on the runway that Concorde then ran over. The plane was a DC-10, registered N13067, which was based at the company's Houston hub.

The DC-10 is an elderly aircraft, about the same age as Concorde. In aeronautical circles, it is regarded in a very dim light. The industry learnt a lot about aircraft safety by not doing what Douglas did with the DC-10.

Problems included a major design flaw with the cargo door, which led to one of the greatest scandals in modern aviation. The design error meant luggage handlers would sometimes believe a cargo door to be properly closed when it wasn't. As a result, a number of passengers died after being sucked out of a DC-10 mid-flight. The problems were eventually resolved but many lives were lost before it was fixed. Even when the American Federal Aviation Administration (FAA) knew of the issue, it chose not to ground the DC-10 fleet immediately.

But this time it was a maintenance problem, rather than any inherent design defect, that led to disaster. During a standard procedure, some wear strips for thrust reversers had been changed. These are thin lengths of stainless steel that often need replacing. But instead of using the material specified in the manual, titanium was used. What's more, they also got the thickness wrong.

Had the DC-10 been properly maintained, the wear strips would doubtless have stayed in place - and not ended up sitting on the CDG runway ready to damage the tyres of a passing Concorde.

∞∞

The second BEA report emerged in December 2000.

Those who had hoped for a major revision were to be bitterly disappointed. The document contained many updated paragraphs and half a page of corrections, but it was largely focused on telling the history of previous Concorde tyre-related incidents, and did not properly explore the reasons for the actual crash.

But at last the missing spacer was mentioned.

It appeared among a paragraph of notes on the undercarriage inspection.

The spacer was listed in some bullet points over three lines - and then quietly forgotten about in all the analysis and conclusions.

∞∞

The missing spacer was not the only mistake made by Air France staff. There were many other errors, some of which contributed to the disaster.

Most of the passengers for flight 4590 had made their way to Paris on short flights from Germany. At check-in, their baggage was recorded on an electronic baggage reconciliatory system, whose job it was to associate each piece of luggage with a passenger and ensure that passenger and bags flew together. This was a simple but effective security system, designed to prevent terrorists checking bombs onto flights that they had no intention of boarding.

But despite the computer system, a staggering 29 items ended up in the plane's hold without ever having being recorded as Concorde-designated luggage.

Weight had always been a major issue for Concorde. Even hand luggage was weighed when a passenger checked in. But the operational error meant these extra items were left unaccounted for, unnoticed and unweighed in Concorde's hold. The extra luggage tipped the scales - the bags meant the aeroplane was definitely overweight. The luggage further hampered the crew's efforts in trying to wrestle precious seconds of flight on their way to Le Bourget.

ᔕᔣᔢ

The Air France crew also made some serious mistakes that day. Before pushing off, Captain Marty had signed a load sheet. It showed an allowance of two tonnes of fuel for taxiing. But when he was about to take off he discovered only 800kg of this had actually been burnt, leaving Concorde over its maximum permitted take-off weight. Marty would have known the manual clearly stated a take-off must not be attempted in these circumstances - the weight limits were absolute and not to be exceeded for any reason. But to the great surprise of the many Concorde pilots who analysed the crash, the take-off attempt continued.

Even worse, the crew did not follow one of the first and most basic rules of aviation - when fully loaded, an aircraft should always take off into the wind.

When air traffic control gave the crew their wind reading - 8 knots from 090 degrees - they should have immediately requested a few minutes to check their calculations and then taxied to the other end of runway 26 Right to take off into wind. If they had done this, Concorde would never have crashed.

But none of this was done. The crew prepared for take-off, overweight and in the wrong direction. By flying the wrong way down the runway the Concorde crew effectively added yet another two tonnes of weight to an already overweight plane - they were now way over the maximum permitted structural weight.

The engines were fired up and Concorde started its take-off attempt. The aeroplane then hit the deadly metal strip, which burst a tyre and the aeroplane started to career off the side of the runway. As soon as he discovered he was heading for the grass, the pilot should have been using everything at his disposal to prevent a disastrous runway excursion. But for some reason - which would never be explained - Marty failed to straighten up: he utilised only one half to two thirds rudder.

The failure to use the full rudder was extraordinary, particularly bearing in mind the potential for a collision with a Boeing 747.

The flight data also showed that Marty raised the nose very early. Supersonic pilots were always trained to avoid an early rotation (or nose up). Climbing too early or with insufficient speed was very dangerous, partly because of the unique aerodynamic properties of Concorde's unusual delta wing. Critically, a low-speed climb would create unusually large amounts of drag, and reduce the potential for speed - and altitude - once in the air.

An early rotation was therefore to be avoided, almost at all costs.

But the nose was brought up far earlier than the crew had agreed. One of Concorde's early test pilots remembers the dangers of this only too well. "In one of the original Concorde test flights, a pilot brought the nose up early when we were simulating an engine failure. Initially we couldn't even get beyond 25ft above the runway."

The early nose up also meant Concorde lost the benefit of its nosewheel steering, further hampering the crew's ability to keep the aeroplane on the tarmac. In the end, Concorde took off at the very edge of the runway and her undercarriage wheels destroyed a runway edge light as she lurched into the air.

Of course, Marty's problems didn't even stop there. Seconds after the early take-off the fire alarm on Engine 2 sounded. Marty immediately asked for the "Engine Fire Procedure" and in so doing set in motion a string of operations for his crew to perform. The engine throttle lever was pulled back and the fire handle pulled. This isolated the engine and shut its thrust down for good.

The decision to shut down an engine so early was also rather surprising. British Airways and Air France pilots were told to avoid an engine shut-down in the early stage of flight. Every ounce of thrust was required before and immediately after take-off. Only once a height of 400ft had been achieved was a functioning engine to be abandoned - even if it was on fire.

Although there was ambiguity in official procedures, the Air France manual did state, "In case of a failure on take-off, no action will be taken before 400 feet AAL [above the runway], apart from ensuring the track and gear retraction".

When Engine 2 was shut down early, Concorde's crew were left overweight, underspeed and underpowered. As she headed towards Le Bourget she was in serious trouble. Concorde would get no faster than 210 knots during the entire flight - and according to the manual the engine shut-down meant she needed some 220 knots to safely stay aloft.

So were Air France's maintenance, operational and cockpit mistakes a dreadful one-off?

Not exactly. Regrettably, Air France does not have quite as good an operational record as its British cousin.

Since it was formed in 1973, British Airways has lost six aircraft. A 747 was blown up in Kuwait by Iraqi forces, a VC-10 was written off after an in-flight failure and two Tridents were lost due to mechanical failure. But other than a mid-air collision, which was due to poor air traffic control, the only loss of life on BA was the 1985 Boeing 737 disaster in Manchester.

Air France has lost some fourteen hulls in the same period. Among these was an A300, where parts of an engine blade shattered sending shards of metal flying through the fuel tanks, causing a fire.

A tyre also burst on a 747 while taxiing, causing a fire that consumed the airframe. Amazingly, there were no casualties.

The most disturbing event was witnessed in 1994, when an almost brand new Airbus A340 was rolled out of a hangar at CDG after an Air France A01 check. While being taken to the terminal to load up with passengers, it suddenly burst into flames and was lost.

It doesn't take a mathematician to work out that such occurrences may be more than statistical anomalies.

The Concorde which crashed in Paris was not the first supersonic airliner that Air France had managed to damage either. A few years earlier, an Air France pilot made a terrible landing at Dakar airport in Senegal. The tail-wheel was crushed and the rear of the engines scraped down the runway for several hundred feet, twisting the metal as the plane ground to a halt. The ruined craft had to be ferried back to France for repairs before it could be used again. It was eventually broken up and used for spares.

∽∾∽

The final report emerged in January 2002. Details of the missing part now stretched to six pages.

Most of this was used to demonstrate that the spacer was definitely not on the plane. The rest was designed to prove that its absence didn't matter anyway and couldn't have had anything to do with the crash.

⤳ oⱱɔ

But was the missing spacer really so irrelevant?

In the two flights before the crash, the lack of a spacer meant that the shear bushes - whose job it was to keep the axle properly aligned - were shaken out of position. Under normal use in taxiing, the pilot would have been blissfully unaware of the problem. The basic geometry of the plane would have kept the bogie running straight, just as a supermarket trolley's wheels follow each other without needing to be connected.

Indeed, were it not for the burst tyre, Air France would have got away without the missing spacer. After a few more flights the undercarriage leg would have started to get damaged by the missing bushes - and at that point the problem would have been detected and the part replaced.

But the tyre burst made the problem far more complex. Some industry professionals disagree with the BEA - they are convinced the lack of a spacer meant Concorde's wheels came out of alignment as soon as the tyre was lost. If this did happen, the aeroplane would have become very difficult to control. Captain Marty would have been battling to control the equivalent of a huge broken supermarket trolley at nearly 200 knots. There is certainly some evidence to support this theory - particularly the kilometre of tyre skids.

John Hutchinson, a retired BA Concorde pilot, is one of those to point the finger at the spacer. "The fact that the skid marks were present on only one side suggests that the spacer played a critical role in forcing the aeroplane off the side of the runway".

But the French investigators and some other experts continue to dispute such theories, claiming the engine's asymmetric thrust was what was responsible for the aeroplane heading towards the grass. The French team provided a theoretical model in the final report to support their theory, which apparently showed the loose shear bushes could not prevent the bogie from running true. There was a critical problem with the analysis. It completely neglected the effect of the bursting of tyre 2, the very reason why a skew could have taken place.

The BEA report also showed there was no skew when Concorde had four fully inflated tyres during taxiing and before Concorde reached V1 speed. But it was what happened to the alignment *after* the tyre burst that really mattered. On this issue, the BEA remained silent. To compound matters, the BEA's final report made little attempt to explain the four-way skid marks left by the skewed bogie, photographs of which they had kindly included in their report.

Eventually, long after the final report was published, a test would be carried out as part of a French judicial inquiry, using one of Air France's other Concordes. This apparently showed the spacer was not to blame. But it was highly improbable that the test duplicated the exact conditions on the day, in particular the burst tyre, the engine variations – and the weight being over the regulated maximum.

∽∾∾

The British investigation team were appalled by the report. In an official response, the AAIB complained that they had been refused access to key parts of the wreckage – even the recovered cockpit instruments. They had also been prevented from properly examining the metal strip and associated tyres.

The British also claimed the French action had been in direct contravention of the Chicago Convention and the European Council Directive 94/56/13 which states, "Investigators should be able to complete their tasks unhindered."

The French had also subverted the directive's requirement that "air safety requires investigations to be carried out in the shortest possible time".

Alan Simmons' team were also worried about one of BEA's key theories - that a piece of tyre striking the wing had caused a shockwave to reverberate around the fuel inside the wing, which in turn forced a section of the skin to fall outwards. According to the French, this explained a piece of wing which had been discovered on the runway.

The BEA had gone to some lengths to prove this theory. A full-sized replica of Concorde's wing had eventually been built - a complete mock-up of exactly the same dimensions. Pieces of rubber were then fired at the fake wing, to show how the symptoms could be reproduced.

But however many times they tried, the BEA hadn't been able to duplicate the effects that they had predicted. Not liking the results of their expensive experiment, the French team created a computer program that simulated the sequence of events in its own virtual world and, conveniently, the computer reproduced exactly what they wanted to see. The AAIB were unconvinced.

∾∽∾

The official report had left one critical question unanswered. Why hadn't Concorde been able to reach Le Bourget for an emergency landing?

The amateur video footage of Concorde's final flight, which was broadcast on every major TV news programme worldwide, gave the impression that the crew and passengers had had almost no chance of survival.

But in reality, Marty and his crew had very nearly made it. The plane's wing structure certainly remained relatively cool during these critical moments. The tonnes of fuel on board kept the wing temperatures down, even as flames followed behind. And most importantly, for a long time Concorde continued to generate the engine thrust required to stay aloft. What the crew and passengers needed was to get to the runway, where a fire crew was waiting to greet them, ready to spray foam on the burning airframe.

In the end, the reason for the crash was the failure of the already struggling Engine 1. When this failed there was no way a disaster could be averted – the crew had already shut down Engine 2 early, and lost the benefit of its thrust. Microscopic accident analysis after the crash would show Engine 1 had ingested a very hard substance, which included some steel. Sadly, the source was quite possibly the runway edge light which Concorde had run over.

This simple object, which Concorde's crew should have been able to avoid, may well have helped kill off the engine and its thrust.

⌘

The crew who died so tragically on 25 July 2000 were very experienced, the élite of Air France. The situation they were put in was also uniquely challenging and so it is not surprising that they were treated as heroes in France following the tragedy. Nevertheless, there must remain some serious concerns as to their actions that day. They allowed the aeroplane to take off over its maximum structural weight, in the wrong direction, brought the nose up early, failed to use full rudder to avoid a collision – and turned a critical engine off early.

Of course, there is no certainty that Concorde could ever have made it, even if procedures had been followed to the letter. And even if they had, they would certainly have had a bumpy landing – and the aeroplane would have been threatened by a raging fire.

But the distance to Le Bourget was short: the flight time was less than a minute. If they had reached the airport, there would have been a very real chance of at least some passengers making it out alive.

Some will argue that this could never have happened. Those who have trawled through the flight data are forced to keep an open mind. A lot went wrong. A lot was preventable.

❧

It may seem distasteful to examine human error, particularly since all those aboard - including the crew - tragically lost their lives.

But these days, air accident investigators increasingly focus on human error when an accident happens. There is a simple reason: you need to make sure it can't happen again. After all, a crew's failure to adhere to procedures can be a mere one-off event - or it can be a symptom of wider problems within an airline. So such issues need to be investigated fully.

So of the hundreds of pages in the accident report, how many were dedicated to the crew's handling of this particular disaster? Less than four. This was quite insufficient considering the scale of the disaster and the number of errors made.

❧

But with the publication of the report, the French investigation had at least drawn to a close. The manufacturers could now try and get Concorde's reputation back together.

The document's primary recommendations focused on reinforcing Concorde's wings and tyres, making Continental audit its maintenance procedures and forcing airports to improve runway inspections. Out of some dozen paragraphs, only two carried any mention of the spacer and other mistakes, and then only indirectly. There was a request for an audit of some Air France practices - but the significance of the operational, maintenance and cockpit errors was brushed under the carpet.

❧

The press reported the investigation's findings at face value - and Air France's senior management breathed a collective sigh of relief. The travelling public would remain largely oblivious to the mistakes that had been made.

The French nation was also left blissfully unaware of another key fact: how close they had come to losing their president. The final accident report diagram of the runway had been carefully drawn. While detailed, the choice of scale meant that Chirac's endangered 747 was just off the page – and did not have to be pictured.

So how close had it been? According to those present on the day, the burning Concorde had come within seven metres of a deadly collision.

To Fly or Not to Fly

Chapter 10

A phoenix flies again

... a new beginning? ...or the beginning of the end?

"There were doubts last night over whether Concorde,
the world's first supersonic jetliner, would ever fly again,
after safety experts prepared to withdraw its
certificate of airworthiness."
The Guardian, 16 August 2000.

∽∘⌣∾

It wouldn't be easy to bring Concorde back. Airbus Industries, the ultimate successor to the plane's original manufacturers, wouldn't be that interested. After all, there could be no more orders - Concorde was a plane from the past.

Air France's management was also uncertain. The tragic deaths had shocked the airline. Perhaps it was best if she was quietly retired.

But the British national carrier wanted their supersonic flagship back. BA knew they would have to keep the pressure up - and in November 2000, some months after the first BEA accident report, the British Concorde team called a crisis meeting. The venue was London's Gatwick airport and the topic was simple - should Concorde fly again?

∽∘⌣∾

Everyone who had ever had anything to do with Concorde turned up. The meeting was far too crowded to make any sensible decisions. Even within each organisation there were many opposing opinions.

So BA's Jim O'Sullivan dragged away the people who could really make it happen - the specialist engineers from BA, Air France and Airbus. They quickly concluded it would be possible to prevent another tragedy. The main concern was the cost of the changes.

The CAA and French air safety regulator La Direction Générale de l'Aviation Civile (DGAC) would need to approve any modifications. Design details would need to be scrutinised, new components tested to destruction.

Would the airlines agree to such a heavy investment? It would be an uphill struggle. The engineers decided to try.

What probably kept Air France in the game were its engineers. The accountants may have been praying for a permanent grounding. But the technicians had laboured over her for years - and they refused to let the great aeroplane go without a fight.

∽∾∾

The most important requirement would be a replacement tyre. The type in use was decades old. But surely someone could create a better product, given the appropriate incentive?

Concorde's salvation was delivered by Michelin early in 2001 - the Near Zero Growth (or NZG) tyre. It was a radical design, developed following years of innovative research. What ultimately made the new tyre safer was the very outer edge of the tread. Unlike a conventional tyre, it hardly expanded when inflated and hardly deflated when pierced.

Tests were carried out using a piece of sharp metal. When an old-style Concorde tyre ran over it, it burst immediately - usually the testing rig would be out of action for a week. But when the NZG tyre was pierced, it continued to roll, fully inflated. It would last another three simulated take-offs and landings before finally giving up. This tyre was a miracle cure.

There was another bonus - the tyres were lighter than the old versions, which gave the engineers additional weight to play with when considering other improvements.

∾⚬∽

The other big changes were more controversial.

After some discussion, it was decided the fuel tanks needed reinforcement. Any additional weight would have to be minimised - and the internal fuel-carrying capacity needed to be kept near enough the same. The logical choice was a material used in bullet-proof jackets: Kevlar. Trademarked by Dupont, it is a rubber mix that is light, flexible and phenomenally tough.

But behind the scenes, some experts were worried.

In the 1960s, a huge rig had been constructed to test Concorde's fuel systems. It had been a full-sized replica of the wings, without their skin. All the fuel tanks, pumps and piping had been laid out, exactly as in the aircraft.

This enormous test rig was then tilted through steep angles to represent Concorde's climb. The movement of fuel was also monitored during simulated acceleration or deceleration. It was an expensive piece of kit. But it was necessary - the engineers needed to ensure that the engines could never be starved of fuel.

Once Concorde was in service, the rig was dismantled; its task finally complete.

But the Kevlar linings were a modification to the plane's fuel systems. By suspending layers of Kevlar in the fuel, the geometry of the system would change, perhaps significantly. No one had access to the test rig any more - it had long since been melted down. There was no particular reason to think the changes weren't safe. All eventualities had apparently been considered. But in the absence of a full rig, how could anyone be sure?

In addition, when flying at Mach 2, Concorde's skin would get very hot. The fuel in the tanks was supposed to act as a coolant to protect the wings. With Kevlar linings added everything changed. Would this affect the wing's longevity or even fuel utilisation?

Some engineers were concerned. The materials were new – and they had never been used in aircraft in this way before. There was no significant ground testing, either – and no one was proposing building an expensive new test rig.

Instead, the changes would be tested in the air.

∼◦∼

In July 2001, Captain Mike Bannister and CAA chief test pilot Jock Reid arrived at Heathrow.

It would be an emotional day. After Paris, some had doubted Concorde would ever fly again. But now, after weeks of hard work by the maintenance crews, they were about to take a modified Concorde into the sky. How would she perform? And would the tyres and linings work as expected?

Concorde G-BOAF left the shed at Heathrow. An air of excitement gripped the airport. After an extra check by the runway inspection vehicle, the crew taxied for take-off and prepared for the first test flight over the Atlantic.

The press and TV cameras had gathered to see Concorde off – and soon the reporters heard the familiar roar of the Olympus engines once again. She raced down the runway for a perfect take-off.

Concorde was back.

∼◦∼

Fortunately, Concorde's test flights were judged a success. There were some minor issues with the Kevlar linings – but they were all quickly resolved. And on both sides of the Channel, the technical teams became increasingly convinced – Concorde had been made safe again.

BA decided to take further advantage of the grounding – it would refit the fleet. Since the launch of services in 1976, Concorde's cabin had been updated some three times. This time they wanted something really special.

So in an unusual move, BA brought in Terence Conran, the design guru best known for his chain of plush restaurants. Conran was asked to help redesign the fleet's interior together with Britax Aircraft Interior Systems of Camberley. Such was the belief in the plane's revival that some £14 million was spent on pure "comfort improvements", almost as much as the proposed safety modifications.

BA's Chief Concorde Pilot Captain Mike Bannister loved the new interior – but he was also concerned potential passengers might never get to see it. Concorde had received a lot of bad press and might now lose its small but extremely valuable group of frequent flyers. So passengers were kept abreast of all the developments with glossy brochures – and photographs of the work carried out.

A VIP reception was even staged in the Heathrow hangars. Frequent fliers got the chance to watch the modifications taking shape.

BA was pulling out all the stops to restore confidence.

~≈≈~

The work on Concorde's modifications was slow. The linings had to be hand-made because the planes were slightly different from each other internally. But, finally, after months of hard work, BA had three aircraft ready again, enough to restore a passenger service to New York.

Air France was still busy with its own modifications, but the mood there was more sombre. The French were feeling far less confident of the supersonic's future – no budget had been sanctioned for an exciting new cabin refit. The Concordes would fly as before, with the bare minimum of internal work.

Meanwhile, BA geared up for a high-profile publicity push and on Thursday 6 September, Concorde's certificate of airworthiness was restored. According to Mike Bell of the CAA, the plane was now safe again – the likelihood of a catastrophic event was back to "less than one in a billion".

BA's Concorde chief Mike Bannister was delighted. His famous white bird was finally cleared to fly. Commercial services could now be restored.

The following Tuesday a trial flight took place with one hundred BA staff on board. It was a thank-you for all their hard work and dedication to the project.

The flight was a resounding success. Many of the BA staff were getting their first ever chance to try out the Mach 2 experience. BA's employees gossiped among themselves and shared Concorde anecdotes as the plane powered ahead.

But as they flew, the world was changing.

When the BA employees disembarked that day, the terrible news broke. Thousands had been murdered in two burning skyscrapers in New York, and the meaning of aircraft hijackings had changed for ever. Indeed, there were many frequent fliers whom Concorde would never see again. At least forty of BA's best customers had died in the Twin Towers.

As Concorde prepared for her first commercial flights, a new hurdle had appeared: the effects of September 11.

∾◡◠∾

In the aftermath of tragedy, the return to service was delayed. It was not the right time for any high-profile relaunches.

It wasn't until 7 November 2001, some sixteen months after the Paris crash, that Concorde G-BOAF welcomed on board its first paying passengers since the grounding. On the flight were BA chairman Lord Marshall, CEO Rod Eddington and a number of key journalists. Tony Benn, who decades earlier had been crucial in keeping her flying, came down to see her off.

New York Mayor Rudi Giuliani was overjoyed by her return. He welcomed the Concorde service back personally. Boarding the plane at JFK he requested, "Do me a favour, spend a lot of money."

Concorde was reborn, her reputation restored.

For eighteen months the famous supersonic services continued – almost as though Paris had never happened.

Chapter 11

Curtains for Concorde

... and how the supersonics could have been saved

Early 2003 wasn't a great time to be the CEO of a large international airline. Budget airlines seemed to be launched every day. Many of the successful start-ups sold airline tickets for the price of a Big Mac.

As if this wasn't enough, the fear of recession, terrorism and war kept many a business executive on the ground. And then the SARS virus appeared, a deadly epidemic that spread worldwide. Newspapers scared millions with stories of infected in-flight air-conditioning systems. Travellers avoided flying. Ticket sales slumped.

Of course, business travellers had to travel from time to time - not everything could be done by videoconferencing. But cuts in the expenses budget meant the business executive was increasingly sitting at the back of the plane. The first and business-class cabins were almost empty. Losses soared.

Concorde's pilots knew they had a particularly difficult problem. They were flying the most fuel-hungry aircraft in the sky at a time when oil prices were rocketing.

Passenger loads, especially on the French side, were also dropping. On some occasions, Air France had only six paying passengers on Concorde's hundred seats. An unofficial American boycott of French airlines, following President

Chirac's very public tirade against the US-led war on Iraq – compounded the problem. By early 2003, rumours had started to spread – Air France was apparently planning to ditch their supersonic services.

∽∘⌒∘

But what really decided Concorde's fate was a terrifying incident, which took place on 19 February 2003.

An Air France Concorde lost an engine mid-flight across the Atlantic on its way to New York. An engine failure was unusual, but not unheard of.

Unfortunately, the French crew turned off the engine – but left the fuel running. A huge amount of fuel was then lost out of the back of the aeroplane.

To make matters worse, the crew took a while to notice the fuel gauge was dropping at an alarming rate. By the time they did, it was almost too late to get the aircraft to the nearest airport. According to those who had access to the flight data, the aeroplane had only five minute's flying time when it touched down at Halifax International Airport in Nova Scotia for an emergency landing.

Both Air France and Airbus management were shocked – the French had only just escaped another Concorde loss. There had been 56 people on board at the time. Full details of the incident were kept out of the public domain – and secret talks began between Air France and France-based Airbus.

∽∘⌒∘

After this emergency, the French national carrier considered its options once more.

The French government were keen to fully privatise the company – another Concorde crash would have scuppered everything. It was also losing millions of euros keeping its Concordes in the sky.

The planes were burning cash every time they left the hangar.

So when the French airline's officials secretly met with Airbus chief executive, Noel Forgeard, they told him they wanted out – and fast. Clearly, it would be embarrassing if only BA were flying the supersonics. Air France felt the best solution was for all the services to be quietly terminated.

Air France and Airbus were closely linked. Both were based in France. Both had French CEOs. The French government had often helped Airbus financially, Air France had the French government as a major shareholder.

Forgeard told Air France he was all too happy to go along with the airline's suggestion. A closure could mean the Airbus Concorde engineering talent would be freed up for other projects. They could work on planes which could actually be sold, rather than spending effort on a plane which featured only in the dusty back catalogue. In addition, the manufacturer was seriously worried following the most recent Air France incident – the last thing Forgeard wanted was another major accident.

So when BA's Eddington was invited to Toulouse to talk about the future of Concorde, he had a bit of a shock. He discovered Airbus, the company responsible for ensuring maintenance was done to the required design standards, had decided Concorde should be scrapped.

Unless BA was willing to commit over £40 million of extra support money the aerospace manufacturer would refuse to continue supporting the plane, meaning its type certificate, the equivalent of a car MOT, would lapse. If that happened, the CAA would banish Concorde from the skies.

But Eddington had just spent millions of pounds of shareholder money refitting the planes, a decision that had been supported by Airbus. And the Concorde fleet was making very real revenues. He was aghast. Britain's supersonic heritage was being rudely hijacked – everyone knew £40 million of extra investment could never be justified.

The British Airways board considered the issue further. It would be difficult to reverse the decision. Airbus was a very powerful, multi-billion dollar company. BA was highly reliant on them. Eddington could see no way through.

In the end, some financial projections were done. If Concorde was taken out of commission, a good proportion of its passengers would carry on flying – but on existing 747s, and probably seated in BA's first class where there was plenty of spare capacity. Perhaps this was a good way of filling the premium seats, whilst saving millions in fuel and servicing costs.

BA was also aware that Air France could cause trouble. The French had once threatened to lease a few fully-crewed Concordes to Virgin Atlantic, which could then fly out of Heathrow in combined Air France/Virgin colours. The move could have had a devastating effect on BA's business. But British Airways managed to get the plan scrapped. Was there a possibility the plan could resurface? The BA board decided to go along with the closure plan without a fight. They reluctantly agreed to announce the end of services together with Air France, at the cost of £84 million to their shareholders.

The announcement came on 10 April 2003. Airbus, Air France and British Airways issued a joint statement saying that Concorde services were to be scrapped after three decades of luxury travel. BA claimed Concorde was being retired for "commercial reasons, with passenger revenue falling steadily against a backdrop of rising maintenance costs for the aircraft."

The British national carrier also admitted the closure would result in a one-off loss more than four times the amount it had paid for the supersonic fleet twenty years earlier.

At Air France, chairman Jean-Cyril Spinetta said: "Air France deeply regrets having to make the decision to stop its Concorde operations, but it has become a necessity… We are proud to have rallied to this aircraft over the last twenty-seven years."

~∞~

The public was shocked. Concorde had become a national treasure for both countries, gracing the skies of London and Paris on every major state occasion. Surely it couldn't all be over?

Ironically, the first thing to happen after the announcement was a major surge in bookings. Everyone who had one day hoped to savour the supersonic experience realised it was now or never. The credit cards came out and BA took some two thousand bookings in two days. Air France's loads also increased, from an average of 30% to 85%.

The superstars and business executives who had been using Concorde regularly quickly discovered the change in atmosphere. Out went the exclusivity and quiet cabin. In its place came the supersonic tourists, all wanting to take away everything that wasn't tied down. Pilots were quickly forced to ask passengers to leave the safety cards on board - there wouldn't be enough for the return trip otherwise.

The Concorde cabin crew were rushed off their feet. Most seats was now filled with merry enthusiasts, all eagerly taking photos and video footage.

∾◦◦∾

It didn't take long for Virgin Atlantic founder Richard Branson to react. Britain's favourite entrepreneur called in the TV cameras to explain why he was incensed.

He was adamant: Concorde should carry on flying and if BA wouldn't make it happen, Virgin would. The company was happy to repaint the supersonics in its own colours. It would fly them across the Atlantic for years to come. The undisputed king of publicity then offered to buy the entire BA Concorde fleet for just £1. He told the press: "Since the British Airways announcement this morning, we have been flooded with calls from the public, including BA staff, asking us to see if we can keep Concorde flying."

Branson said his long-haul carrier benefited from a lower cost base, which could make the plane work financially, even in the harsh economic climate. Of course, BA and Virgin were arch rivals. They were direct competitors on many of the important intercontinental routes, especially London to New York. Years of hostility had led to expensive court battles and fierce public acrimony. Anti-BA slogans had even been painted on the side of some of Virgin's planes.

BA wasn't going to have its glorious supersonics taken away by Branson - especially for the insulting price of half a pint of lager. They quickly re-affirmed that Concorde was definitely not for sale to any other airline. The supersonics would soon be retired to museums as planned, BA insisted.

❧

But Branson isn't the kind of man to take no for answer, especially from the likes of Rod Eddington, the smooth-talking Australian boss of BA. So Virgin Atlantic upped its bid, accusing Britain's national carrier of "industrial vandalism". Branson said he was now willing to pay up to £5 million for the five aircraft still in use. For this sum, he wanted the landing slots and the other two remaining planes bundled in for free - the extra planes would be needed for spares.

Branson also looked for a compromise. If BA wouldn't sell the planes outright for £5 million, the bearded billionaire would offer £1 million to keep Concorde flying for air shows and public events. He was even willing to go into partnership with his long-standing rivals, if it meant the planes could be kept in the sky.

But BA would negotiate with no one. It confirmed the supersonic passenger services would be scrapped as planned in October, following a brief international tour.

❧

But as the weeks went by, the pressure from Richard Branson and the press became intense. Internet petitions had been set up, calling on BA to save the supersonics and proposing a boycott of its services. National newspapers campaigned to save the fleet.

So BA's CEO Rod Eddington took a second look at the supersonic fleet's fate. Perhaps a limited rescue would be possible? Captain Les Brodie was asked to head an unofficial rescue team. BA also asked the respected Jock Lowe for help and advice. The former chief Concorde pilot had saved Concorde before - perhaps he could do it again.

One idea was flying Concorde at air shows and state occasions, just as Branson had proposed.

Another more ambitious plan was running supersonic passenger flights through a new independent company, which was to be called the Concorde Alliance. BA would provide its existing planes and spare parts for free. Other airlines, potentially including American Airlines, Lufthansa and even Air France would be invited to buy into the company. The French national carrier was even to be asked to consider providing a supersonic aeroplane or two.

BA's new partners would be able to sell supersonic services to their customers and supply feeder flights from European cities. Supersonic flights had been popular with the British public - the new company would promote the experience to everyone in Europe. It was an exciting and bold initiative - and a huge amount of work was carried out internally at BA.

⌒◟⌒

On 31 May 2003 some 58 passengers, three pilots and eight cabin crew boarded Concorde F–BTSD, or Sierra Delta, on the last Air France flight from New York. One of the passengers, an American lawyer, hadn't realised he was flying on such a significant date. He was to end up with a dinner party story he could tell enthusiastically for years.

Everyone on board was highly emotional. As the plane roared across the Atlantic, the passengers walked around, chatting amongst themselves and enjoying the free drinks. The cabin crew soon joined in the party. Passengers lined up in the aisle to visit the cockpit, where the crew obligingly autographed the last supersonic menus ever to emanate from France.

On arrival at Charles de Gaulle, the final paying customers were greeted by thousands of Parisians. They stood on the rooftops and behind windows, all enthusiastically saluting the French pride and joy. Countless Air France vehicles honked their horns as they escorted the plane to her gate. When cabin crew and passengers finally emerged from the plane they discovered an honour guard of pilots, flight attendants and baggage handlers greeting them to cries of "Vive la France!"

"It's very emotional. Concorde is a story of joy, of emotion, of technical prowess," said Jean-Pierre Lefebvre, one of the French crew on board. Pilot Jean-Francois Michel simply noted with regret that his next trip to New York would take "almost eight hours".

It was perhaps unsurprising that Air France chose F-BTSD for the final flight. This particular supersonic held special appeal for the airline - it held the world records for the fastest flights around the world in both directions.

In 1992, she had completed the circuit westbound in just 32 hours and 49 minutes. In 1995, she beat the eastbound record by flying from New York to Toulouse, Dubai, Bangkok, Guam, Honolulu, Acapulco and then back to New York in just 31 hours and 27 minutes.

The French would prefer to forget her other major claim to fame. It was F-BTSD that was once painted blue, thanks to a particularly expensive ad campaign from Pepsi.

∽∾∽

Of the airworthy Concordes, F-BTSD was also the youngest. She had broken the sound barrier only 3,600 times. In effect, she had done the flying time of an eighteen-month-old Boeing 747.

If Air France wanted to keep a Concorde flying for air shows, this would be the one to choose. So industry observers watched with interest for a clue. Where would Air France send her?

The Concorde enthusiasts raised their eyebrows when it was announced that she would be spending her retirement in an aerospace museum at Le Bourget airport. Other than parking her in an Air France hangar, she couldn't be kept closer to home. Le Bourget was also the home of the Paris air show. This was the ideal location if the airline hoped to continue public displays.

So two weeks after her final commercial flight, F-BTSD left her Air France home and flew into Le Bourget, just in time for the 45th Paris show.

It was to be an event charged with irony.

For a start, it was French President Jacques Chirac who stood up to make a public tribute to the nation's favourite airliner. Here was the only president of France to have almost died in a plane crash publicly saluting the aeroplane and airline which had so nearly killed him. F-BTSD was also due to land on the very runway that Marty and his crew had hoped to reach before falling out of the sky.

Those with a long memory would also realise that Concorde was about to make its flight of honour almost 30 years to the day since the tragic crash of the Russian TU-144. And it was doing this at the same show and at the same airport. The pilot was even planning to land on the same runway that the Russian crew had been heading for. The crowds were watching the Concorde display from the same position. It was an extraordinary series of coincidences.

Fortunately, the parallels with the past ended there. The French Concorde landed safely. The airfield quickly filled with the sounds of applause and more cries of "Vive la France!"

F-BTSD taxied to take her place at the nearby Air and Space Museum. For now, there was no official suggestion that she would ever fly again. The public would have to wait and see. The rest of Air France's fleet had also begun their trips to extinction. One flew supersonic - without passengers - to her new home at the Smithsonian National Air and Space Museum in Washington DC. Another was unceremoniously cut up into small pieces to be sewn back together on arrival at Germany's Sinsheim Museum. Others would remain in France.

Air France also had a maintenance depot full of spare parts. Their destination was Christie's Auction house in Paris, where they would be sold off to the highest bidder. The proceeds would go to charity. Lots would even include a spare nose cone, which was destined to be sold for over $500,000.

～◦～

Back in Britain, the BA Concorde fleet was still flying – and seats became ever scarcer as the October retirement deadline loomed.

Sir Richard Branson was still demanding a "summit" to discuss the future of the fleet. He claimed it might be possible to keep the planes flying until 2025. Jeff Livings, Virgin's director of engineering, added that he had not heard of a single technical issue that could not be overcome. "There are aircraft a lot older than Concorde that are kept flying, and they have far bigger spare-parts problems."

Branson had secured some credible backing. John Cochrane, the plane's original deputy chief test pilot, had come out in support: "Sir Richard should be given the opportunity to operate Concorde on the basis that it is an icon that cannot be regarded as the sole property of British Airways."

"They paid a very small price for the actual aircraft. It was a national project supported by the government... Concorde should be kept flying. It is highly premature to start retiring it from service."

Branson's PR blitz had been hitting BA hard. Popular opinion was with the charismatic businessman. But BA wouldn't be attending any Virgin-inspired "summits". All it would tell the public was that it was investigating the possibility of keeping one of the supersonics flying. And to avoid any embarrassment, details of the proposed Concorde Alliance were kept firmly under wraps. Eddington did try to wrest the PR initiative away from Branson, however, by announcing thousands of free supersonic seats on Concorde - which would be offered to the general public.

After years of exclusivity, BA would give everyone the opportunity to experience supersonic travel. The public were invited to enter a draw by telephoning a rather expensive premium-rate telephone number.

∽∾

In Paris the plot thickened. Air France's former Concorde engineers had recently come together to look after the youthful Concorde F-BTSD, now handily situated at Le Bourget Air and Space Museum. The word on the street was that they hoped to enable the plane to remain airworthy, so that it could take to the skies "should this ever become possible at some time in the future".

The French equivalent of the CAA was known to be far more flexible than their British counterparts. So in theory it looked just about possible that Concorde might one day fly again, but only in Air France colours - and only over Paris. Jock Lowe would later note that the aeroplane "could probably be made airworthy in a couple of days".

∽∾

In the final month of BA's supersonic services, interest in the aircraft reached unprecedented levels. Every flight sold out within hours. Concorde memorabilia attracted hundreds of bids on internet auction site eBay. Enthusiast web sites drew millions of users.

For Jetinda Sira, possibly Concorde's greatest fan, it was an extraordinary time. Jetinda had first badgered his father into taking him to Heathrow at the age of six. The journey was long - it took almost two hours to get there, including a fifteen-minute walk to his local train station in Romford, a one-hour train journey to London Liverpool Street, two tube journeys across the centre of London towards Heathrow, and then normally a bus ride or walk at the other end.

But from the moment Jetinda saw Concorde he was hooked. For over twenty-five years he made a regular pilgrimage, eventually travelling to Heathrow three times a week. Unsurprisingly, his father was delighted when Jetinda was old enough to make the trip on his own.

Over the years, Jetinda took thousands and thousands of photos. When Heathrow's security team closed the public viewing areas he refused to give up, resorting instead to long walks around the runway perimeter roads. The key to success here was knowing which runway would be chosen. This required a detailed knowledge of wind directions – and an ability to decipher the transmissions of air traffic control.

Of course, he sometimes missed Concorde's departure or landing due to last minute changes – Concorde wouldn't wait for Jetinda to get to the other side of the airport. On other occasions he was moved on by the police just seconds before take-off. But Jetinda's enthusiasm wouldn't be quashed – and as Concorde's final days approached there were more and more people like him. In the early 1990s there had been around ten plane-spotters watching each flight.

By the summer of 2003 there were hundreds of people peering up at the sky, many of whom came down week after week. The enthusiasts started to swap information on runway movements, often using an internet forum within the popular ConcordeSST.com web site. Friendships were forged.

Jetinda and his friends started to meet at the Green Man pub at Hatton Cross for a series of discussions. It was an ideal spot: very close to the runway perimeter. It was here over a pint that they started to campaign.

They wanted Concorde saved – so they wrote letters to their MPs, and spoke to the press. An internet petition secured over 3,500 signatures.

⤔⤳

Ironically, Jetinda had never flown on an aeroplane in his entire adult life - and he had certainly never been on Concorde. So he was in for a bit of a shock on 3 October 2003 when he met many of his fellow plane-spotters at a popular viewing spot, Heathrow's Esso petrol station.

There in front of him were hundreds of people - and a BBC TV crew, who seemed to be spending most of their time focusing on him. Fellow snapper Sparky (so-called because of his internet nickname) suddenly revealed a British Airways ticket pouch and announced to all present that they had done a whip-round and bought the unemployed Jetinda a Concorde ticket. The television camera captured a speechless Jetinda.

Two weeks later he checked in for his flight of a lifetime. Jetinda didn't hesitate when it came to choosing a seat - it was the back row for him. Finally, after all these years, he would have an opportunity to see those afterburners close up.

Jetinda would never forget his supersonic flight. "I simply didn't believe it was happening to me. I got to fly on G-BOAD, the fastest in the fleet. As soon as I got inside I wanted to jump up and down on my seat. And the flight was so gentle, so smooth. It was completely out of this world."

The champagne flowed - there was a real party atmosphere on board. But as the famous bird headed down towards New York the atmosphere changed. Some of the air stewardesses revealed it was their last supersonic flight. The mood slowly transformed into one of mourning. Jetinda later reflected, "As we reached JFK the whole plane was gripped with sadness."

But Jetinda's surprises weren't over yet. A few weeks earlier he had helped out a young lady plane-spotter, who had had her car towed away by over-zealous Heathrow police. By pure coincidence the pilot on this particular Concorde flight happened to be the father of that very damsel in distress.

So at New York Jetinda's kindness was repaid. He was invited into the cockpit for a tour-of-a-lifetime. He shook hands with the grateful Captain Andy Mills and finally, after twenty-five years of snapping, got to take photographs of the inside of the cockpit.

Jetinda spent just 24 hours in New York, touring the city's sites with Sparky, who had travelled over especially on a subsonic flight. The two friends headed back home on a Boeing 747, a plane which Jetinda affectionately nicknamed "Mr Blobby". The ride back was "very bumpy in comparison with Concorde."

∽∾∾

As the closure deadline approached, BA's Concorde rescue team were running into trouble.

Financially, prospects for a Concorde Alliance looked good. Over the previous six months BA had been making as much as £1 million profit a week from the supersonic flights – and demand for bookings showed no signs of slackening off.

But Airbus' attitude had become more robust. They were now refusing to support the type certificate from the end of 2003 – even if BA wanted to keep the aeroplanes in the sky for the proposed alliance.

BA asked Airbus to consider handing over the responsibility to another company. But French Airbus boss Forgeard refused even to do this, now claiming the aeroplanes *needed* to be grounded. Shortly afterwards, Airbus publicly admitted they wanted Concorde retired. A spokesman claimed, "The planes are old. It is time for them to retire. Everyone has to realise that it is quite normal for planes to be retired after twenty years of service. She must retire."

But it was an odd statement for a company that had until recently suggested the planes would fly until at least 2010 – and which had actively supported BA's decision to invest millions in a costly cabin re-fit.

And one thing was certain. In flying hours, the Concorde fleet was young, very young. Many of the supersonic fleet had flown as little as a two-year-old 747. As for spares, BA had a hangar full of Concordes from which parts could easily have been pilfered.

Jock Lowe would eventually go on record to complain: "We were only talking about a few month's flying spread over five years. For that much flying, you could have cannibalised the other Concordes for spares... But Airbus were unwilling..."

The BA team had one last chance. They asked the British Civil Aviation Authority (CAA) to take a more flexible approach. Concorde was a special case, it was argued. It was a national icon that deserved to remain in the sky. There were enough spare parts available and specialist expertise in-house. The engineers could keep the aeroplane safe. Surely the regulators could make a special exemption to the rules? But after heated debate, the CAA refused to help.

There had been huge efforts made within British Airways. But everyone involved was eventually forced to agree – the game was up. The supersonic programme could not be saved. The rescue team stopped work on the proposed Concorde Alliance programme. Management focused instead on which museums would get a Concorde airframe.

∞⊙∞

Concorde's last passenger flight was scheduled to leave New York JFK before dawn on 24 October 2003. BA 002 was far from a normal supersonic flight – there were certainly no plane-spotters or enthusiasts on this particular trip, despite the fact that many would have eagerly handed over their life savings to secure a seat on the final flight.

Instead the airline invited the rich and famous to board the plane for free. The only paying customers were David and Patty Hayes from Ohio who had bid $60,000 in a charity auction to secure the last pair of paid-for seats. They were the most expensive one-way Concorde tickets in history.

In the airport lounge, guests were shown a video of Concorde's inaugural flight. Many of the crew were in tears – it was a moving moment. The passengers then boarded the great plane for the last time – and the aeroplane headed out towards the runway to a water cannon serenade of red, white and blue.

The VIPs thundered across the Atlantic drinking champagne and sharing jokes between themselves. "What, no more caviar? I'll never fly Concorde again."

For Jetinda and tens of thousands of other Concorde well-wishers the morning had had a very different beginning. It seemed like everyone wanted an opportunity to see her fly for one last time – the British public took to their cars in their thousands.

The roads around Heathrow were gridlocked. Police made life ever more difficult by closing off car parks in an effort to put off the public. Anti-visibility screens were put up all over the perimeter fence, making it nearly impossible for young children to see anything. It seemed to be a concerted effort to make life as difficult as possible for those wanting to say their goodbyes.

But in the end the police stopped moving people on. Every road and every pavement was already filled with well-wishers. Many of the enthusiastic photographers had brought their stepladders. Tens of thousands of videos rolled and cameras snapped as the first of three Concordes flew over to make a perfect landing. The last landing was the VIP flight from New York. From their small windows the Very Important People saw the outpouring of emotion. The merry ex-models, actors and actresses could see crowds everywhere. The traffic had stopped completely – many a driver stood on their car, watching Concorde in awe.

For Jetinda it was a moving moment. For years he had travelled here to see off the great white bird. For a while he had felt a bit unusual – some had even taken the mickey out of his Concorde fanaticism. But here, finally, was the proof that he was right to care. Around him he could hear hundreds of people mourning her demise and wishing they had come down earlier. With Concorde gone, they asked, what was left to make Britain great?

∽✇∽

A week later, BA issued a press release. Here finally were details of Concorde's proposed resting places.

Two aeroplanes would head out to America. One to sit on a barge in New York harbour - the other to live out her days at the Boeing-sponsored Museum of Flight in Seattle. Ironically, the Concorde flying to Seattle managed to secure a special permit to overfly North America at supersonic speeds on her final flight.

Several Concordes would stay in the UK, one at Manchester Airport, one at Heathrow, one in Scotland and one at her birthplace at Filton - the home of Airbus UK.

BA had also decided to send a Concorde to Barbados. Initial concerns over the effects of the salty sea air were allayed when the Barbados government agreed to build a special hurricane-proof climate-controlled shelter for the famous bird.

∽∾∾

Concorde was probably the proudest British engineering achievement of the twentieth century. Everyone in the aerospace industry was keen for BA's airframes to be kept in a good condition for future generations.

But sadly, Eddington's company did not have a perfect track record when it came to preserving the country's aerospace heritage. As the Concorde era drew to a close, another great British aircraft was facing an uncertain future.

Down at Heathrow a team of volunteer engineers had spent twelve years slaving over a British-built Trident 3 aircraft in their spare time. It was a labour of love. With only two such aeroplanes left in the world, she was rarer than Concorde.

On a limited budget, the three friends had tried hard to keep her in a pristine condition. She had also been put too good use. Underprivileged children had often been given the opportunity to tour the cockpit and cabin, through BA-sponsored charity Operation Happy Child.

But unfortunately, BA had also continued to use the Trident for taxiing trials – and so slowly the undercarriage had become damaged. One day in 2003 BA thanked the volunteers by cancelling their entry passes. Shortly afterwards, the company proposed breaking up the aircraft – unless an alternative option could be found.

So what was to become of Concorde G-BOAB, which was destined to remain at Heathrow? Some feared she would replace the scrapped Trident and be used for taxiing or de-icing training. If G-BOAB was to be used in this way it could cause severe damage to the airframe. The Concorde enthusiasts crossed their fingers. The great hope was that she would actually end up in pride of place at the new Terminal 5 building.

∽∾∾

When Jetinda and his friends met at the Green Man a few days after Concorde's last commercial flight they were in sombre mood. Despite all their best efforts the Queen of the Skies was going to be scrapped. They had sent letters to their MPs, to government ministers – even to the French embassy. Almost every letter had remained unanswered.

Some of the aeroplanes would be leaving for foreign lands. They would never return. Within a few months it would be nearly impossible to get any of the famous aircraft back into the air.

For many it seemed like a national disgrace. The cost of keeping Britain's proudest engineering achievement in the sky for future generations would have been small – just a few million pounds. It was paltry compared to the cash spent by the taxpayer keeping the Millennium Dome up every week. Why hadn't National Lottery funds been secured? Why hadn't Rod Eddington tried harder to keep her in the sky?

Of course, BA's biggest problem was always bringing Airbus on side. The French company was terrified of another incident – it wanted no more blotches on its safety record as a manufacturer. And whilst BA had never lost a single supersonic aircraft, the problems experienced by Air France had made Airbus a less than enthusiastic Concorde supporter.

Privately, some of BA's staff compared the safety records. Air France had lost one Concorde, crash-landed another – and nearly lost a third. BA had never lost a single aeroplane – despite flying almost twice the number of hours.

In hushed tones they expressed outrage that the British Concordes were being forced out of the sky by a company based in France – despite BA's perfect safety record. At the end of the day, it was not Eddington but the French CEO of Airbus who had forced the British fleet from the air.

One of Britain's most senior Concorde pilots said, "It was not Airbus' job to kill an aeroplane. It had no business withdrawing the type certificate. Airbus' role was to help maintain an aircraft, not ground it. I do not understand why Rod Eddington told us to celebrate the end – he should have been spending his time jumping up and down publicly about the behaviour of the French. Eddington should have been threatening to buy only Boeing planes in the future. The whole episode was a national disgrace."

⌒⌒⌒

British Airways might have had a better chance of success if it had consulted some specialist lawyers. Airbus' effective monopoly in servicing Concordes could have been exploited by BA. Under European competition law a company cannot abuse a monopoly position – if it does it can be quickly taken to task in the courts.

According to Stephen Hornsby, the respected author of the text book on the subject, *The Competition Act 1998: A Practical Guide,* British Airways would have had a good case. "There are previous examples of such cases. Manufacturers have been successfully taken to task before – and they will be again."

The solicitor added: "Essentially Airbus had a scarce resource - the ability to service and certify Concorde. Competition rules meant that in principle it should have either agreed to provide that service at a reasonable cost - or helped others do the job for them. I feel BA would have had a good case to put before the court."

By applying for an injunction, BA could potentially have forced Airbus to co-operate within days. Others had exploited this legislation to great effect in the past.

But BA failed to use this secret weapon. Instead the British Concorde fleet was evicted from the skies.

Chapter 12

Life after Concorde?

... will we ever fly supersonic again?

When locals heard that a Concorde jet was being transported by road to Germany's Sinsheim museum, the news spread like wildfire. For the last twenty-two miles of the road every bridge, every lamppost, every possible observation point was packed with spectators. It seemed the whole world wanted a glimpse of the final journey of this supersonic wonder.

What they saw was a rather depressing sight. The ex-Air France plane had been stripped of its engines and fin. The outer portions of her wings had been chopped off to help her crawl underneath the bridges. The world's fastest passenger plane was in a seriously sorry state, as she was transported at a snail's pace, her proud flying days clearly over.

For Concorde's supporters it was an embarrassing sight. Was this really the same aeroplane which thirty years ago had been rolled out of the French Concorde factory in Toulouse for a supersonic flight test? There had been so much hope at the time, so much expectation of success.

Had it really come to this?

Concorde may have been buried – but in the end Toulouse itself has not done too badly from the Concorde experiment. It is now the global headquarters of what has become the largest civil aircraft manufacturer in the world, Airbus. Even Boeing has been beaten by this pan-European consortium.

The company has ambitious plans, including the roll–out of what will be the world's largest civil airliner, the Airbus A380. This monster double-decker will seat some 555 passengers for the same fuel costs as the smaller Boeing 747. Indeed, these days, the key objective for Airbus' design team is fuel efficiency rather than speed. It's not terribly exciting – unless you happen to be a financial director of a major airline.

∽ɔᴄ∾

Filton, the British factory where BA's Concordes were put together, has not fared so well. The hangar doors from the Concorde days are still there. And if you look carefully, you can just about see the fading logos of the airlines that once optioned Concorde. They were painted on the Filton hangars to encourage the airlines to convert their options into sales. It wasn't a winning strategy.

The workers at Filton don't build supersonic aeroplanes these days, either. Instead they are manufacturing giant wings from huge slabs of aluminium alloy for the Airbus A380. The once proud British aerospace industry doesn't make complete airliners any more – instead, it makes parts for others to put together.

So is there any hope of a Concorde successor?

At one point it looked as if Boeing might provide something useful. The Americans talked of a Near Supersonic Transport (NST), a plane that could cruise close to the speed of sound, at Mach 0.95. Otherwise known as the "Sonic Cruiser" it would carry 200 people and cut ninety minutes off a transatlantic crossing.

At the time, the press got very excited. Some felt the NST was about the only interesting thing to have come along since the days of Concorde. But the industry experts were unimpressed when they examined the project carefully. Flying at Mach 0.95 was the most inefficient speed possible in flight – far less economical than the Mach 2 speeds of Concorde. The only benefit over Concorde would have been the lack of a sonic boom, meaning the NST could overfly land. But the passengers would have had to pay at least twice as much for their tickets – for a mere 12% reduction in journey time. Boeing eventually cancelled the NST project, blaming the post-September 11 recession. Like Airbus, Boeing's civil aviation division now focuses exclusively on building subsonic aeroplanes.

Of course, Boeing produces more than civil aircraft. It has huge military contracts and also manages the Space Shuttle fleet. This wealth of experience might help Boeing if and when passenger travel ever expands into space – and the company has wasted no time patenting numerous futuristic high-flying vehicles. But the costs of flying faster or higher do not make sense on a planet reliant on oil-based fuels. Until someone gets cold fusion to work the ideas will remain firmly on the ground.

However, there has been progress on a supersonic airliner from one rather unexpected corner.

∽∾∽

In 1994, Cal Jarvis of NASA arranged for some of America's most influential aerospace engineers to fly to Russia. The group, which included representatives of NASA, Boeing and McDonald Douglas, had come for a very important meeting.

The destination was Tupolev's Moscow headquarters, the original home of the Soviet Union's supersonic programme in the 1960s. None of the Americans knew what to expect. Everything in Russia was a bit of a surprise.

Carl hailed an ancient Russian taxi at the airport and stared curiously out of the window as his group escaped the madness of Moscow's overcrowded terminal. Watching the poverty-stricken population outside, they all realised they were a world far away from the plush corporate headquarters back home.

They soon found themselves outside a rather grimy 1960s office building in eastern Moscow, the global headquarters of Tupolev.

They entered through the front door. It took a while for their eyes to adjust – the reception area was dimly lit. Most of the fluorescent tubes had been turned off, presumably to save money. A couple of stray dogs were sleeping in the corner. Some of the group tripped in the darkness.

The onset of capitalism had clearly been a shock - the company's infrastructure was on its knees. But over the next few days, this anonymous office would be the location for a series of extraordinary meetings. The two losers of the 1960s supersonic race, Russia and the United States, were finally meeting to discuss collaboration.

A few days later, the American experts were escorted round an old airfield in the drizzle. Standing in front of an ancient rusting hangar, they waited as the doors were slowly prised open. Finally, the Americans were ushered in. This was the moment they had been waiting for. There in front of them was a production version of the world's first-ever supersonic airliner, the Tupolev TU-144. It hadn't been seen for years. This Communist marvel, originally conceived by Khruschev during the Cold War, had somehow survived.

Indeed, the plane in front of them was the last to have come off the production line - number 77114. The aeroplane sported better engines than the rest of the TU-144 fleet. She had apparently been upgraded at some point and could now fly at up to Mach 2.3. But she hadn't been flown for years, and there were very few people who still knew how to fly her.

～∽～

The Americans were in Moscow because they wanted data. Data for a NASA sponsored supersonic aircraft programme. They had a multi-million-dollar budget to spend - and they wanted to rent a TU-144 for some early experiments.

The Russians had their own continuing supersonic programme too. But a lack of hard currency was slowing them down - a partnership with the Americans looked very attractive.

Over the next few days, many meetings followed. Negotiations progressed and eventually a deal was done. The Russians would supply the planes and crew. The Americans would hand over a few million dollars. The resulting research would be shared between them.

The deal was a good one and the resulting celebrations were riotous. Crates of vodka and Armenian cognac sealed the discussions Russian style.

A few months later, the refurbished TU-144 was back in the air, courtesy of NASA. Nineteen test flights followed.

❧

But Tupolev's cash cow didn't last long. Spending cuts meant the US soon cancelled their supersonic programme – and the Russians were left to continue alone.

Even then, the Russians would not give up. They continued to work, albeit slowly, on a next generation of supersonics. They initially claimed a proposed TU-244 would carry some 300 passengers up to 9,500km using a new exotic frozen fuel – cryogenic gas. The Russians believed gas was the answer to the inefficiencies of the TU-144. Excellent results had apparently been achieved in experiments. Tupolev claimed gas would deliver a 70% saving over traditional aerospace fuel. Of course, it was no coincidence that Russia had the largest untapped reserves of natural gas in the world – the national supplier, Gazprom, had even sponsored some of the new development programme.

But in May 2001, Aleksei Tupolev died at the age of 76. It was the end of an era. The loss of the man who had led Russia's supersonic programme was a real blow for the TU-244. The company initially committed itself to continuing supersonic development work but the programme slowly began to stall. It is now thought unlikely that the new supersonic will ever see the light of day. However, the secretive Russians have surprised the West before – perhaps they will do so again.

❧

There is also the work of French Mirage fighter-jet manufacturer Dassault, which hopes to build a supersonic business jet. The proposed plane would carry five passengers at Mach 1.8, nearly as fast as Concorde. It would also feature improved range compared with Concorde - and a reduced level of sonic boom. This supersonic business jet may yet become a reality. In August 2003, Dassault announced a strategic alliance with Russian military jet manufacturer Sukhoi to create a "common working group".

A US research programme will give Dassault further encouragement. Test flights over the Californian desert showed how the shape of a supersonic jet's nose can reduce the effects of the sonic boom. This research may one day enable supersonic travel to take place overland.

Japan has also kicked off a supersonic research project, which started in 1997. But the NEXST (Next Generation SST Programme) is at a very early stage - the Japanese are only testing small, unmanned model aeroplanes which reach supersonic speeds before falling down to earth by parachute.

But the Japanese experiments have been sufficiently interesting to bring European aerospace giant EADS to the negotiating table. The mammoth EADS is the result of a merger between German DaimlerChrysler Aerospace, the French Aerospatiale Matra and CASA of Spain. It owns a controlling 80% stake in Airbus and through Aerospatiale has a detailed knowledge of the early groundwork carried out on Concorde's development.

In late November 2003, as Concorde's last flight neared, EADS chief executive Philippe Camus suddenly admitted he was considering working with the Japanese to build a 300 seat "hypersonic" passenger jet, which could take passengers from Paris to Tokyo in just two hours - at Mach 4. Unlike Concorde, the new aeroplane would create no more noise than a Boeing 747.

EADS said it had already commenced talks with Japan's trade ministry Miti and was in discussions with Mitsubishi and Fuji Heavy Industries.

The British aerospace industry should not get too excited about these developments. Whilst the UK-based BEA Systems does own 20% of Airbus, the British company has no shareholding whatsoever in EADS. So the workers at Filton could well be forced to watch Concorde 2 take off without them. But there is one glimmer of hope in Britain, the birthplace of modern aviation.

Rolls-Royce's research labs are trying to build an engine with a variable bypass ratio, which would maximise the propulsive efficiency of an engine in all stages of flight. If it works, supersonic travel could become as cheap and quiet as subsonic flights today. This is early-stage work and a commercial application looks like being years away, particularly since EADS is aligning itself with the Japanese engine manufacturers.

Whatever happens, there is a serious environmental issue for every aerospace company to consider: the scarcity of oil. In the next thirty years, oil-based fuels are certain to increase in cost, as global reserves begin to run dry. Supersonic guzzlers won't stand a chance – any supersonic successor will require major technological improvements to succeed. Bearing in mind the technical challenges, the chances of a commercial Japanese/EADS Concorde 2 making it all the way to the production line must be small.

Even EADS chief Camus has been forced to admit that "the market could not currently support the launch" of his proposed "hypersonic" aeroplane.

❧

Looking back, Concorde's designers never realised that passengers would demand more than pure performance. In the 1960s, it seemed speed was everything. But what passengers really wanted was comfort at the right price. Most people will happily spend three times longer on an aeroplane if it will save them £3,000. What probably swung the balance completely was the in-flight television. With entertainment systems in the back of the seat, the subsonic flight didn't seem so bad any more.

Concorde never sported an entertainment system. The speed, the landing, the take-off and the in-flight service were what was enticing. Passengers wanted to savour the supersonic experience.

There is no doubt that the lucky few who have flown on Concorde will never forget the experience - especially as future supersonic travel is unlikely. The two passengers who paid $60,000 to fly on Concorde's last commercial flight on 24 October 2003, could well be the last paying customers to ever board a supersonic passenger jet.

ல்லை

For Londoners, New Yorkers and Parisians, there will be no more opportunities to gaze up into the sky and watch the stunning plane sail by.

And for politicians, musicians and businessmen, the early death of Concorde means Europe or North America will be very much further away. Rock stars will no longer consider popping over to London for a quick gig in Hyde Park, before returning to New York the next day. London's business leaders will also have to forget their frequent day-trips to New York.

In truth, the world has become larger again.

But Concorde was - and will remain - one of the most beautiful and technically advanced aircraft ever built. She achieved so much. She rejuvenated the decaying aerospace industries of Britain and France after the war. She helped turn Europe into the global leader in passenger aircraft.

Let us celebrate her achievements.

She was, and will probably remain, the only successful supersonic passenger aircraft mankind ever managed to build.

Farewell Concorde.

Bibliography

Among the many books and sources on Concorde we read while researching this book, we are particularly indebted to:

Books

Concorde, Philip Birtles, ABC

Air Crash: The Clues in the Wreckage, Fred Jones, Osprey Publishing

Soviet SST: The Techno-politics of the Tupolev-144, Howard Moon, Orion Books

The Concorde Story, Christopher Orlebar, Osprey Publishing

Concorde, John Costello and Terry Hughes, Angus & Robertson, Robert Hale

Concorde: The Inside Story, Brian Trubshaw, Sutton Publishing

Web Sites

www.aviation-safety.net

www.bbc.co.uk

www.ConcordeSST.com

www.unrealaircraft.com

The authors would also like to thank the many aerospace professionals and enthusiasts who gave their time to make this book possible.

www.SupersonicSecrets.com